A Backpacker's Guide To Philmont

By
Bill Sassani

"A Backpacker's Guide To Philmont," by Bill Sassani. ISBN 978-1-60264-242-3.

Published 2008 by Virtualbookworm.com Publishing Inc., P.O. Box 9949, College Station, TX 77842, US. ©2008, Bill Sassani. All rights reserved. No part of this publication may be reproduced, stored in a retrieval system, or transmitted in any form or by any means, electronic, mechanical, recording or otherwise, without the prior written permission of Bill Sassani.

Manufactured in the United States of America.

Dedicated to all those who travel to Philmont
to hike its trails, climb its mountains, and
strive to reach the Summit of Scouting.

Disclaimer

I have tried my best to ensure that the information in this book is both accurate and applicable to the reader. This includes having the manuscript proofread by people who have been Advisors on treks and former Philmont staff. It has also been read by Mark Anderson, Philmont's Director of Program.

However, each year things change. Polices are revised, times are changed, and training or equipment requirements updated. Advisors and crew participants should consult the current Guidebook for Adventure and Treks Book for the most up-to-date information. Once arriving at Philmont, the Ranger assigned to the crew will have been trained in current Philmont camping practices, has a plan for training your crew, and will have opportunities for "teachable moments" which occur informally throughout the crew training process. They also will know best how to navigate through Base Camp and to maximize the crew's time. Their instructions and guidance should be well-heeded.

This book is intended to be a guide, to assist your crew to train and prepare for your Philmont adventure. It is not a point-by-point manual. A certain degree of flexibility is needed not just for attending Philmont, but in any outdoor adventure.

Contents

Appendices

Acknowledgements

WRITING THIS BOOK has been a labor of love, as an opportunity to write about something I care about immensely, as well as to share that love with others. Several people have played a key role in the creation of this book.

First, I would like to thank the person that inspired me to write A Backpacker's Guide to Philmont. Bill Schuler, from Tennessee, was an Advisor in one my crews in 2006. He wanted a publication that he could take back home to refer to when training the crews for his contingent. However, no such publication was available for him to buy. His desire to provide the best preparation for his participants was the catalyst for this project.

My parents, Joseph and Gloria Sassani, have been very supportive of this effort. From the first time I suggested this project they have been my biggest supporters. They also were major contributors to the writing and editing process, and reviewed the manuscript.

PJ! Parmar, a longtime Philmont staff member in the Ranger, Backcountry, and Conservation departments reviewed the manuscript and provided feedback and encouragement for the book. I am also grateful for his words of wisdom regarding the publishing process, his assistance in finding a publisher, and for his friendship.

Mr. Steve Schiffman and Mr. Tom Vande Sandt, Esq., provided legal advice for writing this book, and were very encouraging.

I would especially like to thank the professional staff at Philmont, Keith Galloway, General Manager of Philmont, and Mark Anderson, Director of Program. Mark also read the manuscript and provided feedback to make sure that the book was aligned with Philmont's procedures.

Finally, I want to thank Al, "Mom" Keller. He was the Advisor for my first two Philmont treks as a participant, and was the person who introduced me to the magical mountains of New Mexico. None of this would have been possible without him.

Introduction

EACH SUMMER OVER 20,000 Boy Scouts, Venturers, and their adult leaders travel to Philmont. Considered the "Summit of Scouting" the Philmont experience is known to test its participants both physically and mentally. The process of organizing, training, and participating in a 10-day expedition can be daunting for anyone, especially if one has never been on such an extended trip before. Philmont has its own preferred method of camping and hiking. It also has its own camp culture of do's an don'ts, which can be confusing for the first-time participant.

Even the first few days of a Philmont trek can feel rushed and confusing. There is a lot of paperwork that needs to be in order before hitting the trail. Ranger training is three and a half days long, during which time a lot of information is dispensed by the Ranger, much of which can seem very detail-oriented. From hiking techniques, to campsite setup, even eating lunch must be done the Philmont way.

This book is meant to answer many of the questions you may have in order to enhance your Philmont experience. This is so that you, the participant, will be better prepared when you and your crew arrive at Philmont, and have an enjoyable trek. Although intended for Advisors, the *Backpacker's Guide to Philmont* may also interest Crew Leaders, participants, staff, and anyone else with an interest in Philmont.

A Backpacker's Guide to Philmont was inspired by a conversation I had with one of my Advisors. He wanted more information so that he could better prepare his Scouts for their trek. It dawned on me that there were other Advisors out there who were hungry for information on how to backpack the Philmont way, so that they could adequately prepare their crews. Some councils even stage training weekends at the council camp so that their crews will prepared.

Written from the perspective of a Philmont staffer, this book is meant to be your own personal Ranger, always available to answer your questions and guide you through the Philmont adventure.

Getting Ready for Your Trek

Chapter 1: The First Step

THE CHINESE PHILOSOPHER CONFUCIUS once said, "A journey of a thousand miles begins with a single step." This is most certainly true for your Philmont adventure. There's a lot of preparation that needs to be done so that you and your crew have a successful and safe experience. There is equipment to purchase, reservations to make, crew meetings to attend, and much more.

First and foremost is your mindset. You and your crew must be committed to this experience, and that means putting in the time to train as a group and to get yourself ready for your trek. If you are not committed, then you should not go. I have seen individuals and crews that did not have a fun trek because they did not put in the time at home to practice and to train. My Advisor, Al, who was the lead advisor on my first two treks at Philmont as a Scout, believes in this philosophy. As the council contingent leader, he has every participant sign a contract that states that he/she will attend all contingent meetings and training activities, no excuses. Now that's serious! Consequently, his crews are well trained and organized. Whether your crew is from an individual troop or from the council, the message is the same, take your preparations seriously.

The Crew that Hikes Together, Stays Together

As a crew, there are several things that the group should do together while at home. First and foremost is getting out as a group and hiking together, with full packs.

One option is to do a day hike, with packs loaded as if the group were hiking at Philmont. Group members can carry deadweight to better simulate a Philmont load, which is often 40–50 lbs, depending on one's weight.

Another option is to take an overnight backpacking trip on a local trail. This is more realistic for what you will be doing at Philmont, and will give your group the chance to set up the tents, use the stoves, even participate in the daily Thorns and Roses activity (see the Soft Skills section). You can order trail food directly from Philmont to practice cooking and cleanup.

Practice hikes serve several purposes. They provide the opportunity to practice hiking and campcraft skills that will be utilized while on the trek. The hikes are also a chance to iron out any "speed bumps" of potential sources of conflict. If the crew is used to hiking and working together at home, it will perform at a much higher level while on the trek. Finally, it is an excellent opportunity to get a workout and to get into physical shape for strenuous backpacking.

Shakedown

Do a shakedown before leaving home. Have the crew spread out its stuff in a large circle, with everything out of their packs. The Advisor, or better yet, the Crew Leader, reads off the list of items suggested in Philmont's *Guidebook to Adventure*, while everyone else holds that item up in the air. These items are placed by the crew member in his "take" pile. The second pile is gear that the participants do not need to take, or should not take.

Everyone should have appropriate clothing and layers (preferably wool or synthetics, avoid cotton and denim) for when it gets cold, rain gear, cup and spoon, sturdy hiking boots, and a pack that will fit well and be able to hold all of their stuff plus crew gear. Things that should not go onto the trail include electronic devices such as cell phones, pagers, video games, and CD/MP3 players. Scouts should leave behind junk food and soda, as they will not provide the proper nutrition for hiking, although a group bag of GORP or beef/deer jerky can be a tasty treat in addition to the trail meals.

Please refer to Appendix A for a list of equipment and Chapter 4 for a description of required equipment.

Getting Strong

The most important single thing that individual crew members can do is to be physically ready for the trek. The Scout Oath says to be "physically fit," and those words of wisdom can mean the difference between completing the itinerary, being sent to the Health Lodge, or even sent home.

Focus on endurance and stamina when planning your routine, which may include running, cycling, and swimming, to get your heart rate up. Spend lots of time carrying your backpack loaded with deadweight, such as phone books, weights from barbells, or empty milk/orange juice plastic jugs filled with water. Training with your pack not only gets you physically fit, it trains your body to carrying heavy loads. It also helps you to determine whether or not your backpack is suitable enough to complete the trek.

If you or your participants have been leading sedentary lifestyles, you may have weight to lose. Diet and exercising can do wonders for the waistline, and the less you're carrying around your waist, the more you can carry in your pack. A word of caution: consult with a physician before beginning a diet or workout routine.

Paperwork

Before traveling to Philmont everyone in your crew must have completed the Philmont Physical form and have it signed by a doctor. Be sure that the doctor signs the form (sometimes they forget!) and includes his/her office address and phone number. Staple to the form a photocopy of your health insurance card. If a participant does not have his/her own health insurance, then write "None" on that part of the physical form. Make sure you sign and date the form as well.

Have all necessary paperwork completed before arriving at the Ranch. This includes the crew roster, CPR/First Aid cards, Talent Release Form, and obtaining the BSA tour permit. Keep these documents in a binder or organizer to keep track of everything. Having all your "ducks in a row," will make the first day in Base Camp much easier.

Wilderness First Aid Training and CPR

Starting in 2008 Philmont requires at least one member of the crew to be certified in Wilderness First Aid. The suggested provider is the American Red Cross, which has a partnership with the Boy Scouts. BSA members can be certified by the Red Cross to teach the course, reducing the cost of the course for participants. Visit Philmont's website for more information. In addition, at least one member of the crew, but preferably more, must be certified in CPR.

Remember:

1. Have the right mindset.
2. Do practice hikes as a crew.
3. Do an equipment shakedown.
4. Get fit for the hike.
5. Complete the Philmont medical form and all paperwork: Crew Roster, CPR/First Aid cards, BSA tour permit, Philmont wall map, Talent Release Form, physical forms with health insurance cards attached.
6. At least one member of the crew must be certified in Wilderness First Aid, and one member must be certified in CPR.

Chapter 2: Equipment

THIS CHAPTER WILL COVER the gear that is required for Philmont. It is meant to review the basics and give you a better idea of the gear requirements needed at Philmont.

Backpacks

Your backpack will be your home for the next ten days on the trail. Today's market has an array of packs to choose from, and it can be a confusing process for a first-time buyer. There are two main types of packs, external and internal frame. External frame packs are made from lightweight aluminum with a pack bag attached to the exterior. Internal frame packs have aluminum or plastic stays inside a pack bag to give the backpack shape and support. Both types of packs work well at Philmont. A typical Philmont pack will have a load capacity of 4,000 to 6,000 cubic centimeters.

When loading your backpack, be aware of where the weight is distributed and how it will ride in your pack. With external frame packs, place softer, lighter items, such as clothing, in the bottom compartment, and strap the sleeping back underneath. Heavier items such as group gear should go in the top compartment, with the tent or dining fly strapped on top. Water bottles and smaller items can be stuffed in the side pockets. Internal frame packs need to be packed differently, with heavier items placed in the pack about level with where your shoulder blades are. Lighter gear can go on top and underneath. Always keep important items, such as a rain jacket, first aid kit, water, snack food, where those items can be easily accessible.

The backpack should fit snugly, with the weight distributed between your hips and shoulders. Fitting your pack at home and field testing it during workouts and shakedown hikes will help you iron out the kinks in your pack before you arrive at Philmont. Also, purchase your pack from a dealer, not online or from a catalog. It is easier to make a more informed choice as to which pack to buy when you can try them on, and the store employees can help make adjustments to your pack, such as the waist belt. If you do purchase from a catalog or on the internet, try the item on in the store first to ensure proper fit.

Boots

Next to a backpack, hiking boots are one of the most important pieces of equipment you bring to Philmont. A boot with a leather upper and sturdy sole with tread is recommended. The boot should fit comfortably, with enough room in the toe box for you to wiggle your toes, but not so much that your foot moves around in the boot. However, the boots do not have to be heavy and unwieldy either. If you are unsure as to what would be a good boot to purchase, check the Philmont Tooth of Time Traders website for a list of boots available, then try them on at your local store. This is another item that you should buy at the store, and not online. Wear the boots at home, walking around the house, to make sure they fit. Many stores allow returns on boots if they haven't been worn outside. Check with the store to be sure. Walk in your boots as much as possible to break them in, even to work or school! By wearing your hiking boots while training with your backpack also helps to break the boots in, and gets you used to wearing boots and a weighted pack at the same time.

Make sure that you try on the boots with the socks that you intend to wear while on the trail. Many people use a wool/synthetic wool outer sock and a thin poly-liner sock. This combination reduces friction and blistering on your feet. However, some people are using synthetic-blend socks that do not require a liner sock. Try both combinations, and use whichever works for you. You can also purchase special insoles to provide support or to fine tune the fit of the boot.

Clothing

Philmont's varied climate ranges from a high desert, pine forest, and alpine environments, with elevations between 6,000 feet to 12,441 feet. Temperatures can exceed 90 degrees in the day and drop into the 40s or below in the evenings. Because of this variety, the Philmont trekker needs several different types of clothing to stay comfortable and dry.

One thing to keep in mind when purchasing appropriate clothing is the phrase, "Cotton Kills." When cotton is wet it is very difficult to dry, and the garment will draw heat away from the body. When the weather is hot and dry, this is not much of a problem, but during the famed "Monsoon Season" of mid-July to August it can rain every day, with temperatures being much lower. Clothing made from synthetics will keep the body warm even when wet.

First, let's focus on the clothing next to your skin. Undergarments can be bought with synthetic blends that provide adequate comfort. Some male hikers have found "boxer briefs" to be useful in preventing chafing. For females, sports bras and panties are appropriate. Long underwear can also be purchased made from 100% synthetics, and at a reasonable cost.

A lightweight pair of shorts and a t-shirt is appropriate for summer hiking days. The innovation of the zip-off pant allows you to have both a pair of light weight shorts and trekking pants in one garment. A t-shirt is appropriate for wicking away sweat. Philmont not only sells t-shirts, but will also customize silk-screen shirts with the Philmont logo and your crew number. Discourage participants from wearing sleeveless shirts, as this exposes a lot of skin to ultraviolet light and sunburn. If you're shoulders are sunburned, it can be very painful to carry a pack.

A hat or cap with a brim keeps the sun out of your eyes, and wicks sweat away from your brow. A "boonie" hat with a 360 degree brim will help protect the neck from sunburn.

To stay warm, carry one or more insulating layers, such as a fleece or wool jacket or sweater. A knit or fleece hat will also be helpful for keeping you warm. If your hands tend to get cold easily, a lightweight pair of gloves is recommended.

Shell layers are worn over insulating layers. These are garments made from lightweight, breathable nylon that will keep you dry from the rain and allow moisture from your body to evaporate. A sturdy rain jacket and pants combination work well, and can be fairly inexpensive to purchase.

Clothes worn during the day can contain salt stains from sweat, food odors from cooking, and food particles, which could attract a bear. Thus, you will need a set of sleep clothes for the evening. A pair of gym-shorts and a t-shirt work well, as you may need to wear these clothes while walking from your tent back to the packs to store your day clothes, due to lingering food smells. Pack an extra set of clothes in resealable plastic bags to change out of in case clothes get wet or lost/destroyed.

Sleeping Systems

Believe it or not, there is a system to sleeping in the backcountry. The two main components are the sleeping bag and pad. The sleeping bag keeps you warm, while the sleeping pad provides comfort and insulates your body from the ground. Without it, more of your body heat would be sucked away by the cold ground. That could mean the difference between a good night's rest and a fitful evening of shivering, especially at higher elevations, such as Mt. Phillips Camp or Copper Park Camp.

Choose a sleeping bag that you find comfortable, and that is easily packable. Synthetic bags work well in wet environments, but can be heavy. Down sleeping bags, made from goose feathers or other feathers, work better in dry climates and are more lightweight, but if they get wet they can be difficult to dry, and can make for an uncomfortable night's sleep.

Sleeping pads vary from closed cell foam pads to inflatable, lightweight backpacking mattresses. Both work well, and can be bought in varying sizes such as full-length, ¾ length, and ½ length.

Here's a trick for your sleep system: stuff clean extra clothes, such as a rain jacket or extra fleece, in the sleeping bag stuff sack at night to make a comfortable pillow. You'll sleep more comfortably, plus your extra layers will be ready if you need them, and you will save the weight of carrying a camp pillow.

Eating/Drinking

A lightweight bowl and spoon made of metal or plastic will be required when eating Philmont meals. There is no need to bring a knife or fork, although some campers like to use "sporks," a spoon/fork combination utensil. A plastic mug is great to have for hot drinks in the evening, and especially for Advisor's Coffee at staff camps. Make sure to mark your utensils to prevent confusion.

Water bottles are needed to prevent dehydration. Each participant should have at least three, 1-quart water bottles. Mark the bottles so everyone knows which belong to whom.

Hydration systems have become popular in recent years. These are water bladders with a drinking tube attached that allow the user to drink without having to stop to pull out a bottle from the backpack. If members of your crew want to bring these, make sure they have at least one water bottle, preferably a wide-mouth, for drink mix. Also, hydration systems sometimes get punctures in the bladders and leak.

Smellables/Toiletries

"Smellables" refer to any items you carry that are made by humans and have a smell. These are items that would attract an animal, such as a squirrel or a bear. These items are collected each evening and hung in bear bags over steel cables, out of the reach of critters.

Below is a list of such items. They include...

- Food
- Trash
- Soaps
- Tootpaste/toothbrush
- Medications
- Wipes/sanitizers
- Feminine hygiene products, used and unused.
- Empty Philmont bear bags
- Clothing with large amounts of spilled food or blood
- Sunscreen
- Insect repellent
- Chapstick/lip balm
- Water bottles that have drink mix, or have had ever had drink mix, in them
- Disposable cameras
- Extra film roles and canisters

It may seem strange to think that disposable cameras, film, or sunscreen may be smellables. However, in the past bears at Philmont have been attracted by these items, and have wandered into campsites.

When organizing smellables, each crew member should have his own small stuff sack or resealable bag with their smellables. Label or otherwise mark the bags to prevent confusion. Do not let participants store non-smellable items, such as compasses and flashlights, in their personal sack, or spread loose items around in the backpack. Money, despite what some crew members may think, is not a smellable.

Other Items

- 10–12 large resealable bags
- Ground cloth for tent
- Camera with film
- 50 feet of parachute cord
- Book
- Journal and pen
- Pre-stamped and pre addressed post-cards
- Fishing license-can be purchased at Philmont Trading Post
- $10-$20 in small bills-for buying extra shots for rifle or shotgun shooting, or a cup of root beer at the cantina.
- Flashlight/headlamp
- Extra batteries

Group Gear

These are shared items for crew use. Philmont provides cook-sets, dining fly with poles, tents, and water purification tablets. If a crew wants to use their own tents/fly from home, they may do so. The following are group items that should be brought by the crew from home:

- Well stocked first aid kit.
- Water filter with replacement filter
- Backpacking stoves
- Fuel bottles
- Parachute cord for dining fly ridgeline
- Repair kit
- Tent stakes

Purchasing Equipment

As mentioned earlier, you should purchase your backpack and boots from a store that specializes in outdoor retail. However, many of the other items on the Philmont packing list can be obtained from discount stores, military surplus, or borrowed from others for the trip. Check with others from your troop who have been to Philmont, or if you're in a council contingent, the contingent leader or council high adventure committee. Wherever you get your gear, make sure you try everything out before you leave home to make sure it fits and works.

Remember

1. Buy boots and pack from a store for the best fit.
2. Choose synthetics for warmth and easy drying.
3. Keep a separate resealable plastic bag or small stuff sack of "Smellables."

4. Buy items from discount stores or on-line to save money.

5. Try out everything before leaving home.

Chapter 3: Traveling to Philmont

JUST GETTING TO PHILMONT can seem like an expedition in itself, no matter which mode of transportation you choose to get there. Those that drive use personal vehicles, troop vans or buses, and even chartered coaches. Crews that take the train arrive at the Raton train station where Philmont busses can take you the rest of the way to the Ranch. The crews that fly arrive at Denver, Colorado Springs, or Albuquerque, then take chartered busses or rental cars to Philmont.

When traveling, keep these things in mind. Leave the white gas at home, fuel can be purchased in Base Camp for the first few days on the trail, and refilled at commissary camps in the backcountry. Fuel bottles must be empty and aired/washed out, without the smell of fuel in them in order to mail. If flying, all U.S. Transportation Safety Administration rules must be followed, such as regarding sharp objects, liquids, etc. My Advisor, Al, also tells his crews, "Do not say bomb or gun when in the airport, even if you're joking." Good advice.

Sightseeing

If you have the time, do a little sightseeing before arriving at Philmont. Many Scouts have never been to the West, so it can be a real adventure. There are lots of options, such as whitewater rafting, touring museums, visiting the Air Force Academy, or Native American pueblos, taking a tram to the top of Sandia Peak or Pike's Peak, etc.

Another benefit to sightseeing is that the participants can have more time to adjust to the dry climate and higher altitude of the Rocky Mountains, as many crews come from sea level. Even though there is little physical activity during this time, crews should still be drinking lots of water to prevent dehydration. They should also apply generous amounts of sun block, as the sun is brighter in the West.

Advisor Al also has a trick when traveling with large contingents. Feeding seventy Boy Scouts can be a chore, and if the whole contingent goes to the same fast-food restaurant, it will take forever for everyone to get their food and get back on the bus. Instead, he has the driver stop at an exit where there are several fast-food restaurants to spread out the load. This way everyone can get their food and be back on the bus in a reasonable amount of time, and they get some variety.

Because so many crews opt to sightsee, packaged deals are available. Companies will now pick you up at the airport, take you to see the sights, and drive you to Philmont in coach busses. This takes away some of the guesswork for you when it comes to making arrangements or accommodations.

No matter how you decide to travel or where you go, remember that your crew or contingent is representing the Boy Scouts of America to the public. People have certain expectations as to how Scouts act and be- have. This means that the group needs to be on their best behavior at all times. Use the Scout Oath and Law as your guide. Also, be- cause your group is traveling as part of a BSA official function, they should be dressed in the Scout uniform. Many crews wear their full Boy Scout Uniform, which includes the tan button shirt/Venturing shirt, green shorts or Venturing shorts, belt, and Scout socks, when in the airport. The crews change into crew shirts t-shirts, with the official shorts and socks, when sightseeing or travel- ing on the bus.

Remember

1. Ship fuel bottles clean and empty.
2. Follow all TSA rules for travel on air- planes.
3. Add a couple of days to sightsee and acclimate.
4. Packaged tour programs are available.
5. You are representing the best of the BSA to the public.

Chapter 4: Arriving at Philmont

AS YOUR BUS DRIVES SOUTH from Cimarron to Base Camp, look to your right to see Baldy Mountain and Touch-Me-Not in the distance, while buffalo cluster near the fence bordering the road. The bus passes Tooth-of-Time Ridge, then on the left the Villa Philmonte, Waite Phillip's summer mansion appears, with large cottonwood trees lining the road. Finally, you pull into Base Camp, a large sign, "Welcome to Philmont-Beinvindios!" greets you. At last, you have arrived!

Below is a guideline for getting through Base Camp. This process is not considered an exact science, and some degree of flexibility is necessary. Your Ranger will know best how to get your crew through this process.

Checking In

The lead Advisor or Contingent Leader should go into the Welcome Center office to let the staff know your group has arrived. If your group has arrived after 5 PM, the staff will assign tents in trail-bound tent city, which is on the far side of Base Camp. Otherwise, your Ranger will meet you at the Welcome Center after getting your tent assignments from the Welcome Center office. Have the Crew Leader introduce everyone in the crew to the Ranger, so that he/she can begin to learn your names.

The Tents

After your Ranger has led you to your tents, your crew can drop their bags in the tents. Don't get too comfortable though, because there is a lot more to do. Crews often take a few minutes to change out of travel clothes and to visit the restrooms. Everyone should have a filled water bottle, a rain jacket, and any prescription medications with them. A school-sized backpack can be handy for walking around Base Camp. The lead Advisor/Contingent Leader should have all the group paperwork including the completed crew roster, BSA tour permit, CPR/First Aid cards, a Philmont map, Talent Releases, and completed medical forms.

While staying in Base Camp tents keep all food or other smells out of the tents to discourage mice, squirrels, or skunks from paying a visit. Store group food and smellables in either the crew lockers or personal vehicles overnight.

Registration

The Ranger and lead Advisor go into Registration, while the rest of the crew and Advisors wait outside. A crew toy, such as a hacky-sack, can be a great way to kill time. The "Hurry Up and Wait" philosophy will be a recurring theme this day.

In Registration, the office personnel take your crew roster and tour permit for filing. They then take the Advisors back for a meeting while the Ranger goes over to Logistics to get a spot in line for the trek briefing.

Logistics

This is where the Crew Leader and two Advisors meet with a Logistics staffer to review the trek. Each day of the trek is plotted out on the map, where the crew gets water, picks up food, completes their conservation project, picks up burros or ride horses, and when their scheduled to be return to Base Camp. The rest of the crew and the Ranger usually wait outside the office or at the Trading Post snack bar pavilion. It takes about an hour to get out of Logistics, so the Ranger may utilize this time for training and getting to know the crew.

Health Lodge

At the Health Lodge everyone's medical form is reviewed by one of the recheckers. Each person should have prescriptions, including inhalers and epi-pens, ready to be inspected by staff. Anyone who is 18+ will have their blood pressure checked. If your blood pressure is too high, the staff will ask you to come back later to check again. Note that if your blood pressure is still too high or your height/weight does not fall within Philmont's parameters, you will not be allowed on the trail.

While your crew is waiting, your Ranger may take the time to do some training, such as first aid, map and compass, or getting to know the crew better.

Services

This is where your crew is issued tents, dining fly, cooking equipment, bear bags. and water purification. It's also where your first few days of food are issued. If you get tents and a dining fly, they must be hung on the bungees and visually inspected for holes or missing poles. Many crews choose to bring their own equipment instead of using Philmonts.' Services is also where one can find the packs and gas room, drop off or receive mail, crew storage lockers, and telephones. Callers need prepaid phone cards in order to use these phones, and the do not accept incoming calls.

Shakedown

After Services typically is shakedown. The Ranger may ask to meet you at your tents, in front or behind services, or a grassy area with all of your stuff. The Ranger will have your crew spread out your gear and he/she will read off from a checklist. You hold up each item, then place it in a pile.

Trail food and group equipment commonly taken on a trek. Make sure to check for damaged gear or meal bags that are punctured before leaving the Services building.

There will be a pile of stuff to take and a pile of stuff to be left behind. If the crew has already done a shakedown at home, there should be few surprises. Personally, I focus on what's in the toiletries kit, as there's always one person who wants to bring deodorant on the trail. See the appendices for a complete packing list.

A Philmont Ranger conducts a shakedown. This helps the crew to lighten their load, as well the Range and Advisors to be sure that everyone has what they need for the trail.

27

Security

Security is located between the Welcome Center and News/Photo. This is where keys can be picked up for crew lockers, and is where Lost and Found items are stored. If your group arrived by private vehicle, Security will have you store travel baggage in your vehicles. This is to save crew lockers for those who flew out and do not have any other way to store their baggage. Keep in mind these lockers are small, so avoid having an excess amount of baggage.

News and Photo

News and Photo, also known as NPS, is where crew photos are developed. The photos are usually taken at a tarp in between Trailbound and Homebound Tent Cities. Photos can only be taken in the morning, because afterwards the sun is no longer behind the camera.

It is best to wear the full BSA uniform or matching crew t-shirts for photographs. Glasses and sunglasses need to be removed so that everyone's face can be clearly seen. Warn crew members not to make gestures or funny faces, as the photo is a souvenir for everyone in the crew.

Meals

All meals are taken in the Dining Hall. Crews must have their meal tickets for the Ranger to give the Dining Hall Steward. These are obtained from Registration when

you check-in. Tradition dictates that the Rangers will sing the Ranger Song before each meal. The Rangers then line up to hand over the meal tickets, and will call their crews over to the appropriate entrance. Usually each crew recites the Philmont Grace before entering the building. It goes, "For food, for raiment, for life, for opportunity, for friendship and fellowship, we
thank thee O Lord. Amen."

Meetings

The Crew Leader, Advisors, and Chaplain's Aide all have meetings after dinner at 5:45 PM. Everyone heads towards the Advisor's Meeting Room (AMR) and are separated to their respective meetings. The Crew Leaders get a talk from a member of Ranger Leadership as to their job responsibilities, being leaders, and what Thorns and Roses is. The Advisors are briefed on various topics ranging from potential forest fire danger, dehydration, special trek opportunities, and more. The Chaplains Aide meets with a member of the Chaplaincy Corps to learn more about their role in the crew, the Philmont Duty to God patch, and learn about Thorns and Roses.

Religious Services

The hour between 7 PM and 8 PM is designated for Chapel. The Trading Post is closed during this time, and quiet time is observed in Base. Crews can choose to attend Catholic, Protestant, LDS, or Jewish services. If it rains, alternative accommodations are arranged. Catholics will meet under the covered area for medical rechecks near the Health Lodge, while Protestants go to the Sliver Sage Staff Activities Center. Those attending the Jewish services usually go under the covered area of the chapel, while LDS services are already held in a roofed building.

Opening Campfire

The final step for the day is attending the Opening Campfire. It's a good idea to bring something warm to wear and carry a flashlight for the walk back to Tent City. The crews walk across the street to the Opening Campfire Bowl, led by a member of the Activities Staff. The campfire takes about an hour.

The Next Day

If your bus is scheduled for the first run of the day, then your crew must have their packs packed at the Welcome Center, tents swept and clean, and travel bags in storage *before breakfast*. The Registration Office opens before busses leave, which lets you drop off keys and important papers for the safe. Then it's time to load up for the backcountry! Note that the busses arrive early, so make sure your crew is at the Welcome Center 15 minutes before your bus is scheduled to arrive.

For bus times later in the day, you will have more time to make final arrangements. However, the Welcome Center likes to have crews out of tents early in the morning to make room for new crews arriving that day. If your crew arrived in the afternoon the day before, you may still have to finish checking through Base Camp before your bus time.

Scramble, Be Flexible

The check-in process at Base Camp can be stressful and frustrating. Just remember the old Ranger saying, "Scramble, be Flexible," when things seem to be getting out of hand. Thankfully, you only have to spend your first and last nights in Base!

Remember

1. Advisors check-in at Welcome Center.
2. Meet your Ranger.
3. Drop stuff at tents. Each person gets 1 H2O bottle, rain gear, prescription medications. Advisor has Crew Roster, CPR cards, BSA Tour Permit, Talent Releases, medical forms, and Philmont map.
4. Advisors and Ranger check-in at Registration.
5. Crew Leader and Advisors trip plan with Logistics staff.

6. Health Lodge meets with each participant, goes over medications, and checks
blood pressure of anyone 18+.

7. Services issues food and equipment. It
is also where Packs/Gas, Mail Room,
and crew lockers are located.

8. Shakedown

9. Security for locker keys.

10. Meal tickets are required for Breakfast, Lunch, and Dinner.

11. Advisor, Crew Leader, Chaplain Aide
meetings are after dinner.

12. Chapel services at 7PM, quiet hours.

13. Opening Campfire meets at Welcome
Center.

14. Next day catch the bus to the backcountry!

Hard Skills

"Hard Skills" is the term used by Philmont to refer to the technical knowledge needed to complete a trek. This includes knowledge of backpacking, campcraft, first-aid, Leave No Trace awareness, and a number of other skills. The Rangers teach these skills during the first three and a half days a crew is at Philmont. It can be overwhelming soaking in all this knowledge in such a short period of time, that's why you have this book as a resource!

Chapter 5: Off the Bus

YOUR CREW HAS LEFT Base Camp to the trail-head, gateway to the backcountry. Finally, you're on your way! During the ride, your Ranger points out various historical and natural landmarks, as well as spins some tall tales and corny jokes. When you have arrived at the turnaround, and unloaded your packs, the Ranger directs you to a shady spot under a tree to begin training. As the crew walks over, you may turn your head around to see the yellow school bus already driving away, leaving a large dust cloud in its wake.

The Ranger typically will cover four things before the crew begins hiking. These include map and compass skills, going to the bathroom, putting on packs, and hiking etiquette.

Map and Compass

Maps

When navigating during hikes, it is helpful to use Philmont sectional maps. They are more accurate and show more detail than the full wall map used for trip-planning at Logistics. Spread the sectional map on the ground, and look at the different topographical features.

The first thing that should stand out is that there is a lot of green on the map. Green represents forests, or vegetation that is over six feet tall. The next prominent color is white, vegetation that is below three feet tall. In some areas there are green and white splotches, which is vegetation between 3–6 feet tall.

Learning about map and compass, including map symbols, orienting the map, declination, triangulating, and UTM coordinates.

Blue represents all water bodies. Lakes, ponds, and streams that always have water in them will be solid blue. A dashed blue line represents a lake or stream that is seasonal, and only exists if it has been raining. Sometimes a lake will be solid blue with a larger blue-dashed line surrounding it. This means the lake is always there, but when it rains can expand to the size of the blue-dashed line. Natural reservoirs will appear in the form of small blue circles. In the southwest corner of Philmont there are marshes, which are blue tufts of grass and water.

Anything black on the map is man-made. These include grid lines, buildings, roads, trails, wells, mine shafts, and place names.

Contour lines are brown. Contour lines represent differing levels of elevation. The number of feet between each line is the contour interval. On the Philmont wall map the contour interval is 80 feet, while sectionals will be 40 feet.

On maps there will be a legend to identify different things on the map. There will also be a diagram that tells the reader the adjustment to declination. Declination is the difference between True North (North Pole) and Magnetic North. The declination at Philmont is approximately 9 degrees 3 minutes to 9 degrees 15 minutes east. A scale at the bottom of the map helps determine distance.

Compass

There are many varieties of compasses, but most have similar features. A compass will have a base plate, which will have a direction-of-travel arrow on it. On top of the base plate is a housing containing an arrow, the red part of the arrow points north, the white south. Circling the housing are num-

bers that can be turned. At the bottom of the
housing is the red outline of an arrow.

Orienting to True North with Map and Compass

To orient the map to True North, lay it
flat on the ground. Then take the compass
and turn the housing to line up to about 351
degrees with the direction-of-travel arrow.
Lay the compass lengthwise on the map,
along the black grid lines. Then, turn the
map until the "red is in the shed," with the
red part of the magnetic needle lined up with
the red arrow outline on the base of the
compass. When this occurs, the map is oriented to True North, and can be used for
navigation. Note that on Philmont sectional
maps the declination is 9 degrees, 3 minutes.
This can change over years so be sure to
check the declination icon on the map.

Shooting Bearings

Take the compass and aim the direction-
of-travel arrow toward a prominent feature,
such as a mountaintop. Turn the compass
housing until the "red is in the shed." Then
go back to the map, and place one corner of
the compass on the turnaround labeled on
the map, and line up the other end until "red
is in the shed." The compass should point
towards the prominent landmark. Do this
twice more, marking each bearing with a

line. Where the lines intersect is your location. If the triangle formed by the lines is very large, then you may be off on your bearings and should reshoot them. If the triangle is small, then you're on target.

Grid Coordinates

Your Ranger will at some point review how to read grid coordinates. This is an important skill, as it will be necessary for you to provide your exact location in the event of a medical emergency or if your crew spots smoke from a forest fire.

Grid coordinates at Philmont are read using the Universal Transverse Mercator (UTM) system. Similar to latitude and longitude, UTM divides the earth into vertical and horizontal lines, allowing the user to pinpoint a location on the planet. To use UTM with the Philmont map, find a point you want to identify, such as a camp. Then look on the sides of the map and the bottom, you should find numbers that identify the horizontal and vertical lines.

Next, find the vertical line that runs top-bottom on the map which intersects the camp. This will be your first number. For the second number, follow the horizontal line to the side of the map. Most of the time camps do not fall on the exact lines. To get the exact numbers, divide the grid square into tenths. Follow your finger up from the margin to the camp. Repeat for the horizontal line. A grid coordinate will look something like this: 505000 x 4023000.

The grids can be broken down into smaller units for getting a more exact location. There are tick marks in between each grid number, with each tick mark a unit of 2 (2, 4, 6, 8, 10). Imagine that your location is between 505000 and 506000, such as Rayado Camp. Rayado Camp will be 505900. Repeat this process for the vertical number, which is 4024800.

During your trek, practice orienting the map, shooting bearings, triangulation, and grid coordinates to master these skills. Ask your Ranger to help and to provide clarification.

Going to the Bathroom

After about an hour of reviewing map and compass skills, as well as drinking lots of water, it will be time to go to the bathroom. When urinating, go 100 feet away from trails, roads, and water sources. Urinate on the ground, either on dirt or pine duff. The urine will quickly evaporate, or will be licked up by animals for the salt in the urine.

Typically there will be latrines at the turnarounds, so the Ranger will lead the crew on a "latrine tour." Everyone gets inside the latrine, while the Ranger talks of the finer points of latrine use. Before using the latrine, open the lid and wipe the inside lid with the end of a stick to get rid of cobwebs and spiders. After use, dispose the stick away from the latrine, and remove your unused toilet paper. Do not urinate in the latrine, as this will prevent the breakdown of waste. Do not throw garbage or food down the latrine, or vomit into the latrine, as these will attract bears.

There are other latrines on Philmont, including unwalled "pilot to bombadiers" and "pilot to copilot" latrines. There will be times though when there will not be a latrine, especially if your trek is in the Valle Vidal, where such structures are not permitted. You will have to dig a cat-hole to dispose of your waste. Go 200 feet from trails, road, and water sources, and dig 6–8 inches into the soil with the crew shovel. This is the layer of soil where microorganisms will break down waste. Use a small amount of toilet paper and leave it in the hole with the waste, then cover the hole with the dirt. Never let the shovel touch the waste, and do not burn toilet paper, as this may start a forest fire!

Always use a hand sanitizer after visiting the latrine to prevent the spread of disease. Whole crews have become ill because someone did not wash his hands after visiting the latrine.

Loading Packs

Once everyone is refreshed, it's time to get the packs on. Some Scouts will try to play the tough guy by swinging their packs onto their backs, but this method can result in injury. Instead, lift the pack and rest it on your hip, then slip your arms through the straps, and slide the pack on. Snap the hip belt, with the belt resting on your hip bone, then adjust the shoulder straps. You also can have someone lift the pack up, straps facing out, so that you can slip the pack on without stressing your back.

Hiking Etiquette

The last topic to cover before hiking is etiquette. There are a lot of people who use Philmont trails, and there are specific things a crew must do in certain situations. Knowing the "culture" of Philmont is just as important as knowing the technical skills taught by your Ranger.

Passing

If you encounter a crew ahead of you when hiking, and it looks like you will overtake them, ask the crew for permission to pass them. It's inconsiderate to hike up right behind a crew and force them off the trail. By giving a loud warning, such as, "Permission to Pass!" lets a crew know that there's someone behind them, and that they should move off to the side of the trail.

When hiking downhill, such as off the summit of Mount Phillips going down to Clear Creek, if you see a crew going uphill, let them pass. This is considered a courtesy, as people hiking uphill must use more energy to stop and then start hiking again. Of course, some crew members may desire any excuse for a quick rest, but you should still make the offer.

If your crew is on a road, such as the stretch from Ponil to Sioux camp, step off the road for vehicles. Make sure that your group is on the driver's side so that the driver can see you better.

Philmont operates burros and horses on its trails, and often, crews encounter these pack animals. If your crew sees another crew with burros or a group on horseback, they should ask the animal's handler or Wrangler what to do, and when in doubt step as far off the trail as possible, and downhill if practicable, so that the animals will not consider you a threat. Speak to the Wrangler or the rest of the crew in normal voices. Loud voices or sudden movements may startle the animals.

The rule here is courtesy. When in doubt, step off to the side.

Group Hiking

When the crew is hiking, members of the group should be spread five to seven feet from each other. This is so everyone has some space to view the scenery, and is not bunched up so close that one has a backpack in his face or bumps into the person ahead of him. Also, look up and around, enjoy the scenery. Most participants have their eyes focused on the ground, and they miss out on the Philmont beauty.

During the hike, the Pacesetter is in the front of the line. This person, or persons, has the ability to set a pace that everyone can keep up with. The ideal pace allows everyone to talk without feeling out of breath. Sometimes crews see the Pacesetter as the weakest member of the group, someone who is slow and out of shape. This could not be farther from the truth! The Pacesetter has a very important job, to make sure the group stays together while still getting to the destination. Either a Scout or Advisor can be the Pacesetter, whatever works best for the crew.

The next person in line is the Navigator, sometimes jokingly referred to as the "naviguesser." This is the person with the crew map and compass who determines the route for the day, and advises the crew as to which trail to take. This job is rotated around so that each Scout will get a chance to be the navigator. The rest of the crew with the Crew Leader follows the Navigator. The Advisors often hike in the rear, unless the group decides that one of the Advisors should be the Pacesetter. If the crew has a Ranger, he/she will hike behind the rest of the crew. This is as symbolic as it is practical, as the Ranger's job is to teach the crew, but to also empower the crew, particularly the Scouts, to be the leaders and make the decisions. See the Soft

Skills section for more on crew responsibilities and interactions.

A crew hikes past a beaver dam on their trek.

Finally, before setting off on your hike, hoist your water bottles into the air in a toast for good hiking. Then the Pacesetter asks, "Is anyone not ready?" This is to identify who in the crew is not prepared to hike, instead of assuming that everyone is ready to go. If someone isn't ready to hike, he should inform the crew, so that the whole crew can leave together. If no one responds, then it's time to Hike On!

Remember

1. Identify the different parts of the map and compass.
2. Know the difference between True North and Magnetic North.
3. Orient the map to True North using the map and compass.
4. Shoot bearings to triangulate your position.
5. Determine your exact position using grid coordinates.
6. Urinate on dirt or duff.
7. Know how to use latrines.
8. Know how to dig cat holes.
9. Load packs safely to prevent injury.
10. Courtesy is key in the backcountry.
11. Know the roles of the Pacesetter and Navigator, and rotate these roles among the crew members.

Chapter 6: The First Day's Hike

HIKING ALONG THE TRAIL for the first time can be a wonderful experience, as the crew leaves the hectic pace of Base Camp and the "real world" behind, and begins its' Philmont adventure. It is a good feeling to know that all of the work and stress from a year's preparation is paying off, and that you actually are hiking at Philmont. The first day is also a learning experience, as this is the first time the crew is hiking at elevation with full packs. Many participants breathe a little harder and break into a sweat earlier as they carry a full load of food, water, crew gear, and personal equipment.

The Tyrannosaurus Rex footprint, which crews can visit on their first-day hike to Anasazi Camp.

Your Ranger is going to use this time on the trail as another teaching tool for your training. Throughout the first day's hike there will be plenty of "teachable moments." These are opportunities for you and your crew to learn various tricks for hiking, as well as pearls of wisdom regarding how to deal with certain situations on the trail.

Trail Signs

Trail signs help participants navigate Philmont backcountry trails. They are made of wood with place names routed onto boards that are bolted to wooden posts. There are three kinds of trail signs. Signs with flat ends

One of the three ways to identify a campsite is the number block, which is usually attached to a tree near the fire ring.

mark a location, such as a camp. Signs shaped as an arrow are directional signs, indicating where a trail leads, such as the trail to Sioux camp. If a trail sign has arrows on both ends, it means that you are in the middle of something, such as a canyon. Unlike other parks or forests, there are few named trails on Philmont.

A Philmont trail sign. Remember the Four T's: not to Touch, Turn, Trust, or Tinkle.

Rangers teach the "Four T's" for trail signs: Touch, Turn, Tinkle, and Trust. Do not Touch a trail sign, as salt and oils from hands will be left on the wood, and will attract animals, damaging the sign. Never Turn a trail sign, even if you think it is pointing in the wrong direction. Do not Tinkle on a trail sign, that is, urinate on it. Again this is because the salt in the urine will attract animals, and also because it's unsanitary. Finally, do not Trust a sign, as it may have been Touched, Turned, or Tinkled on! Always use your map and compass to confirm your route at major intersections. If a trail sign appears to be damaged or you believe it is pointing the wrong way, mark it on your map and report it to the nearest staff camp.

A trail sign points the way at Old Abreu camp, a typical first day starting camp for crews.

Stream Crossings

Many streams and rivers cut through trails at Philmont. Some are so small that one can easily step over these rivulets and continue hiking. However, larger streams require the crew to stop and cross purposely.

Most of the larger streams have footbridges installed for crossing. They are usually two logs that have been leveled on top and anchored to the stream-bed. Others have planks hammered into them and have reinforced steel cable anchors in case of flash floods. The footbridge just before Abreu Camp, and the one crossing the Cimarron River at Bear Canyon are two examples.

To cross the bridge, each participant crosses one at a time, while the next in line waits for the Scout ahead of him to reach the other side. Everyone waits for the last person to cross, making sure there is enough room on the other side for everyone to step off the bridge. The Pacesetter asks, "Is anyone not

A participant crosses a stream by stepping over rocks. The crew waits for everyone to cross before hiking on.

ready?" If there is no answer the crew continues hiking.

When crossing these streams it is recommended that you undo your waist belt and loosen the shoulder straps. This is in case you accidentally fall off the bridge and into the water below. The extra fifty pounds that you're carrying can quickly pull someone underwater, especially if he has been knocked unconscious. If crossing a stream without a bridge, do not cross is the water level is above the knee and/or is moving quickly. It doesn't take much water for a hiker to lose balance and fall. Use a trekking pole to maintain balance.

Gates

Philmont maintains miles of fence line to control animals, including its cattle herd. Wire gates have been established where trails and gates meet. These gates have the same strands of barb wire, usually 4–5, as the rest of the fence, and are attached to a wooden post that can be removed from two wire loops tied to a fencepost.

To cross through a gate, the pacesetter opens the gate by lifting the post out of the loops and pulling the gate to the side. The rest of the crew walks through the gate and waits on the other side. The pacesetter pulls the gate back across the trail and places it back in the loops, then rejoins the group. The question is asked, "Is anyone not ready?" and if there is no response the crew continues hiking.

Sometimes a gate will already be pulled back and tied with wire to the fence, holding it open. If your crew finds a gate in this manner it is okay to leave it as is. The Philmont cowboys and often leave gates this way when moving cattle or horses to different pasturing areas. If a gate is found lying in the trail, then someone either did not place it correctly back in the wire loops, or just left it on the ground. You can do your "Good turn for the day" by placing the gate in the correct position.

Breaks

Trail breaks are an opportunity to take a swig of water, to adjust packs, and to rest. There are two kinds of breaks, those that are less than five minutes long and those that are fifteen minutes or longer. Short, five minute breaks are good for checking the map, getting a quick drink of water, or taking a picture. If you wait longer than five minutes, then lactic acid begins to build up in your legs, which can cause cramping. Short breaks can be unplanned, but a rough time-frame can be one every forty-five minutes. Any more than that, and your crew should consider a longer break.

Rest breaks that are fifteen minutes or longer allow you to take your pack off, rest, to take care of foot problems, and to eat lunch. This gives your body time to flush out the lactic acid in your system. Breaks such as these can be planned into your hiking day to take advantage of nice views or points of interest. As an example, your crew could plan a thirty-minute lunch break at the pond on Wilson Mesa when hiking from Sioux to Pueblano. There is plenty of shade, and a great view of Baldy Mountain.

Lightning

Lightning procedures are taught by your Ranger in the event of a severe thunderstorm. If you see a lightening bolt, start counting, "One-one thousand, two-one thousand, three-one thousand, etc." When you hear the thunder, you can estimate the distance from the strike to you. Every count of five is a mile. If you hear thunder before the five-count, especially if it's an instant flash-boom, then you and your crew must get into the lightening position quickly.

Spread the crew members out, so that there is about 30 feet between each person. You should be able to see the person in front of you and behind you, but not the front and back of the line. Take your backpack off, and set it away from you and sit on a foam pad, with feet on the insulating surface. The insulation will protect you from ground current. The ideal position is crouching on your haunches, with your arms crossed over your knees and ankles touching. It can be difficult to maintain this position for a long period of time. A modified position is sitting on the pad with arms crossed on upright knees, ankles touching. Ditch trekking poles as far away as possible, as these may attract electricity.

The Ranger will demonstrate these positions to the crew, and will have them practice. It is a good idea to do a simulation drill so that everyone knows what to do when the real thing happens.

At almost every turnaround, it is possible to cover most of these teachable moments during your first day. Don't let the crew get into the mindset of focusing on getting to camp. Take advantage of these opportunities to learn as much as you can from your Ranger, and to ask questions. Remember also to keep drinking water and to check your feet for hotspots or blisters.

Remember

> 1. The four T's of Trailsigns: Touch, Turn, Tinkle, Trust.
> 2. Cross bridges one at a time, wait till everyone's across.
> 3. Wait till everyone is through a gate and the gate has been closed.
> 4. Take breaks to hydrate, enjoy views, and have meals.
> 5. Know the lightning position and have the crew practice it.

Chapter 7: Campsite Setup

ARRIVING AT CAMP after a long hot day of hiking, it can be tempting to throw down the pack and kick up your feet. But there's still a lot to do, and it takes the whole crew to get the job done right. Here are the steps for establishing your campsite when arriving at a trail camp.

Campsite Map

When arriving at a camp, such as Lover's Leap Camp, a campsite map will be readily noticeable from the trail, nailed to a tree. This map is made from Geographical Information System (GIS) data collected by Philmont, and is very accurate. Marked on the map will be numbered campsites, sumps, bear bag cables, latrines, and water sources.

Study the map, then a few Scouts should go ahead up the trail to check out the sites. If there are no other crews in camp, then the courteous thing to do is take a site that is in the middle of the camp. This is so that when crews that come into camp late in the day can take the first camp immediately without having to spend precious daylight looking for a site. A campsite will have three things, a number block nailed to a tree, a metal fire ring, and a sump for grey water disposal.

Once the Scouts have found a desirable site, they can return to get the rest of the crew.

First Things First

When setting up camp, it can be tempting to set up your own tent, crawl inside, and take a nap. Rangers teach that all crew chores are to be completed first before setting up personal tents. These chores are, in order: bear bags, dining fly, crew gear, tents.

Bear Bags

Setting up bear bags and hanging smellables is the first crew chore because it is desirable to get all food off the ground as soon as possible. The crew should gather together all food and personal smellables into the bear bags, including any empty bear bags, as well as the bear ropes. Once all the bear bags are ready, bring them over to the bear cables.

The bear cable is a steel cable that has been bolted into two trees about fifteen to twenty feet off the ground. They are designed to hold several crews' worth of smellables, and have been placed so that there are ample trees to tie off to.
To hang the bags, first uncoil the rope to loosen any knots and tangles. There should be one overhand loop knot at the center of the bear rope. Recoil the rope loosely so that you are holding the two loose ends in one

hand, with the knotted middle coiled up, or, you can wind up the knotted end into a baseball. Throw the rope over the cable, with your back towards the trees you intend to tie

Bear bags hanging from a bear cable. Note how the bags are close together. Bags that are spaced far apart hang lower, which makes it easier for bears to reach.

off to. The knot should be hanging close to the ground. Be careful if the knot gets stuck in the cable, and try to carefully work it loose. Many crews have to cut their bear ropes because the rope got twisted around the cable, causing it to form a girth hitch when pulled from below.

Next, take one of the bear bags and twist it to form a narrow neck at the top. Take the rope and make a lark's head knot. Fit the knot over the bag neck until the knot meets the body of the bag, and cinch tight. Tie the other bags to the bear rope in this manner, keeping the bags close to the center knot and evenly weighted on each side.

A lark's head knot is used to tie bear bags to the bear rope. Note how the bag is tied close to the center-loop knot, which helps to keep the bags in a tight cluster when raised.

After the bags have been tied, rig the "Oops Bag." This is the bag intended to be an emergency-use bag, in case someone finds a forgotten candy bar or wrapper in their pocket later in the evening. All one has to do is lower the bag, deposit the smellable, and retie the bag. Many crews use the Oops Bag as an additional bear bag, loading it with so much stuff that its original purpose is meaningless. The bag should have some weight, such as that night's dinner, the group first aid kit, or a full water bottle. This will make it easier to raise and lower the bag.

Thread either the spare bear bag rope or parachute cord through the loop and tie the extra bag on one end. A climbing-rated carabineer (not a cheap novelty one) is clipped to the loop to reduce drag and makes it easier to pull. Have someone hold onto the loose end of rope as the bags are raised.

After hauling up the bear bags, secure the ropes to a sturdy tree by wrapping the rope around the trunk several times, then wedging the rest of the rope between the first wrap and the tree tree.

When it's time to raise the bear bags, everyone in the crew grabs the two ropes and separates into two groups. Pulling at the same time, the crew pulls back to two separate trees that are in the same general area. Do not split the ropes, forming a "Y," as this will make it difficult for other crews to throw bear lines later. Do not stand under the bear bags while they are hung or afterwards. The bags are very heavy, and there is the possibility that they may be dropped.

Wrap the loose ends of the ropes around two trees several times. You should feel the release of weight as the friction from the rope is taken up by the tree. After several loops around the tree, wedge the remaining rope as a bundle in-between the rope and tree. This will keep the rope secure, and make it easy to untie the ropes later.

A crew checking in to a staff camp learns about program opportunities, what time they start, where to dispose of garbage, and any safety concerns in camp. They are then walked to their campsite.

Finally, raise the Oops bag so that it is part of the larger group of bags. Split the ropes again and tie off to the trees you used for the main bear bags. This method frees up the other trees for the other crews in camp.

Once everything is hung, the bags should look like a tight cluster. If bags are hanging lower than others, as if they were a string of pearls, lower the bags and retie them. The bags should hang just below the cable, so that a squirrel (or mini bear, as they are often called) cannot get into a bag from above. Never tie off bear bags to the same trees that hold the cable. A bear may try to climb these trees to get to the cable, and in doing so will cut the ropes with its' claws. Also, when tying bags in this manner a triangle is formed, making it difficult for other crews to hang their bear bags as the lines will get tangled.

If camping in the Valle Vidal or near Rich Cabins the crew will have to hang bear bags without a cable. One method is to throw each end of a bear rope over a tree limb. The trees should be far enough away from each other so that a bear cannot reach the bags hanging in between them. Tie the bags at the middle knot in the bear rope and rig the Oops Bag. Crew members grab an end and pull in opposite directions. The bag should be in the center of the two trees, and far enough out that a bear could not climb the trees to get to the food. Tie off each end of rope to a separate tree.

Another method is to clip the knotted centers of both bear ropes to a carabiner. Throw the two loose ends from each side over two different trees. Then lift the bear bags and tie off the four loose ends to four different trees. Hang the Oops Bag. This system allows for redundancy if one of the bear ropes snap. However, the carabiner takes on more stress, so make sure it is a weight bearing carabiner.

Dining Fly

The dining fly serves several functions. It is a storage area, an emergency shelter, and a cooking area. It is important to set up the fly so that the rest of the crew gear can be stowed, and to have some shelter available in case of inclement weather.

When picking out a spot for the fly, keep in mind what Philmont calls the "Bearmuda Triangle." This is the area in the campsite where smells are most concentrated: the fire ring, the sump, and the bear cable. This is where a bear is most likely to go when in a campsite to look for food. Because the fly is used for storing food when the bear bags are down and for cooking, it is important to set up the fly in the Bearmuda Triangle. A logical spot is near (but not too close) to the fire ring for easy access to food or cooking gear. The ground does not necessarily have to be flat and level, unlike a tent site.

To set up the dining fly, the crew needs the fly, poles, parachute cord, and six-eight tent stakes. Assemble the first three sections of the aluminum poles, the fourth section is not necessary, as it will make the fly too high.

Next, spread out the fly, with a Scout holding each corner, and one person on each end of the fly. Unroll the parachute cord, making sure that there is enough cord on each lengthwise end to stake out the ends.

Take a loop of cord and thread it through the grommet on each side, and tie a girth hitch knot around a small stick. This puts pressure on the stick, not the grommet. In high winds, the stick will break, causing the fly to collapse, but preventing a rip in the nylon.

Once each end has been tied in this manner, test the cord to ensure that it is tight. Afterwards, take the aluminum poles and tie one to each end of the fly, using either a girth hitch or clove hitch knot. The knot should be tied as close to the nylon as possible for stability.

The two sides can be staked down, using a taught line hitch to secure the rope to the stake. Plant the stake into the ground at a 45 degree angle, with the eye of the stake facing away from the fly. Many campsites have hard, packed dirt or rocks that make this step difficult. Gently press your foot on the eye of the stake, with your hands on either side of the foot, applying downward pressure. Another method is to use a plastic, lightweight hammer, which works quite well. Avoid using a rock as an improvised hammer, as you may damage stakes, as well as leave marks on the rock.

After the ends have been staked down, stake out the four corners by planting opposing corners at the same time. Make sure to use the large loop of rope, not the smaller loop formed by the taught line hitches. To create an even, flat surface on the side of the dining fly, plant the stakes so that the rope "cuts the corner" of the fly. Once this is completed the two sides of the fly may be staked out. Now the crew can place all crew gear under the fly. Backpacks should be stored nearby, not under the fly, during the day so that there is space for the crew if it rains. At night, packs can be kept under the fly when everyone is in tents.

Tents

Once all the crew gear has been taken care of, it is time to set up the tents. Your tent will be your home for each night on the trail, so it is important to put some thought into where you make your bed. There are Five W's that the Ranger teaches for tent setup. These are Wind, Water, Wildlife, Widowmakers, and Weather. When setting up your tent, be aware of prevailing winds by avoiding placing your tent in cross-winds that will blow on the sides of your tent. Do not set up tents where water would drain if it rains, piles of pine needles and erosion are obvious signs. Avoid setting up your tent on game trails or near burrows, and keep your tent 50 feet outside the Bearmuda triangle to avoid bears. Widow-makers refer to dead but standing trees or suspended branches that could fall down onto your tent in strong winds. Weather means setting up tents so they are not vulnerable to storms, lightening, etc. There is also the Wow factor. There are some nice campsites at Philmont, with great views of meadows, mountains, or the plains.

Be aware if your tent is to be pitched on even a small incline, be certain to orient your sleeping bag with your head uphill and the tent door downhill.

A group of tents clustered together to make it harder for a bear to single an individual one out.

If you are using Philmont tents, there are several components. A Phil-tent consists of the stuff sack, tent body, fly, and three aluminum poles. You or your tent mate must provide a plastic ground sheet.

1. Spread the sheet flat on the ground, then empty the contents of the stuff sack on it. Lay the fly on the side and spread out the tent body.
2. Next assemble the poles. Two poles have white plastic ends on both sides, while the third pole has one white

end and a blue cap on the other. The first two poles slide through the sleeves at the tent entrance and connect into grommets at the base, and into the "Air Traffic Controller" or "Tinker-Toy" at the top. This forms an "A" structure. While you are doing this your tent-mate can setup the rear pole. After the poles are set, stake out the front and back ends, and then the four corners.

3. Next comes the tent fly, which uses the same stakes as the tent body for the front and rear. The four corners and four side guide lines are then staked out. Once your tent is up, unzip it to brush out any debris inside, and store the stuff sack in one of the storage compartments so the wind does not blow it away. Do not leave the tent unzipped, as critters may find their way inside.

A Philmont tent requires fourteen stakes "by the book," but you can get away with as few as eight. Typically, only one stake is used for each side for both guy lines. In a pinch, the two stakes that anchor the front can be removed and the poles will still stay upright. Because of the number of stakes needed, as well as for other reasons, many crews carry their own tents from home that are free-standing and require only a few tent stakes. Make sure that the tents have not had food or other smellables in them from previous campouts.

Philmont does not allow participants to use bivy sacks or tarps as shelters. Although very lightweight and functional, these one-person shelters could be mistaken by a bear as a log. Campers in the past have been rolled over by bears looking for grubs and insects to eat. Sleeping under the stars, referred to as "meadow-crashing" is also prohibited for this reason. Shelters also must have a floor sewn to the tent body to prevent snakes and rodents from getting inside and making a nest in your sleeping bag, as well as to prevent the spread of diseases such as hantavirus.

Always pitch tents at least 50 feet outside the Bearmuda Triangle. In some campsites this may be difficult, but do your best to keep the tents and cooking area as separate as possible. Keep tents clustered close together. In the past, bears have been drawn to an isolated tent, and being curious animals, they pounce on them and rip the nylon to get inside. If a camper is inside in the evening, there is the chance for severe injury. Never take food near the tents, and never bring food or smellables inside a tent.

Have at least two participants in each tent. This method reduces the amount of weight each person carries, and also maximizes available space in campsites. If a crew of 10 each had an individual, one-person tent, the campsite would quickly be overcrowded and your tents would be too close to the cooking area.

Concentrated Impact vs. Leave No Trace Hiking

When camping on Philmont property, crews practice concentrated impact camping. Crews stay in designated campsites with established fire rings, sumps, and bear cables. These sites are used every year and receive a lot of impact from hundreds, and sometimes thousands of people staying in the same spot.

Leave No Trace camping methods are used when no such facilities exist. This includes the Valle Vidal, as well as the Double H High Adventure Base. The Leave No Trace program has seven principles:

a. Plan ahead and prepare.
b. Travel and camp on durable surfaces.
c. Dispose of waste properly.
d. Leave what you find.
e. Minimize campfire impact.
f. Respect wildlife.
g. Be considerate of other visitors.

Although crews do practice these principles while on the property, extra precautions must be taken in sensitive areas without designated campsites. When camping, the group must determine its own Bearmuda Triangle, keeping tents 100 feet or more from this area. To concentrate smells, locate your bear bags and sump area near each other.

A crew walks spread apart in a Valle Vidal meadow to reduce impact.

If hiking in a sensitive area, such as one of the large meadows of the Valle Vidal, spread the crew apart so each crew member is hiking side-by-side. This reduces the impact of the crew on the meadow, as only one pair of boots will be stepping on the grass, instead of the whole crew hiking in a line. A path of matted grass would soon develop, and eventually a trail.

When camp has been completely established, the crew can take some time to relax. Participants may want to move sleeping bags into to their tents and to unroll them to fluff up the loft. Others may want to dry out their sweaty t-shirts, air out their feet, read, or write in a journal. Meanwhile, the Advisors can join the Ranger in the celebrated "Ranger Nap."

A typical Philmont fire ring. One of the indicators of a campsite, a fire ring is not only used for campfire, but during a drought it is where the camp stove is placed to cook dinner.

Remember

1. Identify campsite map and scout for a site.
2. Find a site in the middle of a camp to accommodate late-arriving crews.
3. Bag smellables and hang the bear bags.
4. Set up the dining fly and store crew gear inside the Bearmuda Triangle.
5. Set up the tents outside the Bearmuda Triangle.

6. Five W's: Wind, Water, Wildlife, Widowmakers, Wow.
7. You must sleep in some kind of tent shelter with a floor.
8. Have at least two campers per tent to prevent overcrowding.
9. Know the difference between concentrated impact and Leave No Trace camping.

Chapter 8: Cooking and Cleanup

NAPOLEON BONAPARTE, the French general and dictator, once said, "An army marches on its stomach." This is certainly true for Philmont crews. Preparing and eating food that is nutritious as well as tasty is an important daily chore that takes a certain degree of skill. Knowing just the right method for cooking those red beans and rice can make the difference between eating food with texture or eating mush!

Types of Food and Nutrition

Philmont meals are designed to be nutritious, providing approximately 3,000 calories a day. Over the years, different varieties of food have been tried for taste and functionality. For instance, crews in the 1990s ate Pemmican Bars as part of a lunch meal. These thick bars are made from nuts, berries, and molasses, and packed over 400 calories! A great source of energy, they were not always the most tasty food. The only time I could ever choke down a whole bar was if I dipped it in a can of cake icing. Pemmican Bars have been phased out of trail meals to be replaced by an assortment of other energy bars.

Philmont food is mainly carbohydrates, with some protein. Carbohydrates can be pasta, rice, crackers, and sugars. Protein can be found in jerky, dehydrated meat, peanut butter, and nuts. A greater emphasis is placed on carbs because of the need for quick energy, with the protein providing longer-term energy during the day. Dehydrated foods are used to save weight and to reduce cooking time, and everything is pre-packaged for better organization and distribution. One bag of trail food is enough to feed two people.

Some participants have special food concerns, such as being allergic to nuts or wheat, or have religious requirements. Philmont can make accommodations for these participants by shipping replacement or supplemental food provided by the participant to the commissary camps on their itinerary. If this is an issue for your crew, make sure that the participant has brought enough food for the whole trek, and adding in more than you think you'll need is a good idea, as you may underestimate energy needs before hitting the trail. The food should be pre-packed in plastic bags or boxes, with the participants' name, expedition number, and destination written on the outside. These bags will be left with Logistics to be transported to the backcountry. Tell your Ranger about any special dietery needs.

Choosing a Meal

It may feel overwhelming trying to sort through the mess of bags in order to find a meal, so organize them into piles. Each bag has a number on the side identifying which menu it belongs to, such as Lunch #3 or Breakfast #1. Try to eat the meal for the appropriate time, such as breakfast for breakfast, or lunch for lunch. Eating a dinner for breakfast would take a while to cook and may be too filling before setting out for a full day of hiking.

In a pinch though, switching lunch and dinner has worked for crews staying at trail camps that do not have water. This is especially true for crews staying at Tooth Ridge Camp or Schaeffer's Pass Camp on their last night out. Dinner is cooked for lunch at Clark's Fork, then the crew hikes up to camp in the evening with as much water as they can carry. That night they eat their lunch, which does not require any water to hydrate.

Preparing the Kitchen

The kitchen is the area next to the fire ring. Usually logs or rocks surround the fire ring for people to sit on. However, people walking near your food could accidentally kick dust or dirt into the meal, or knock over the stove, causing hot water to spill. Always designate a part of this area as the kitchen, which means no participants allowed!

The cooks should spread out empty bear bags on the ground to hold food packages and to keep them clean. They should have the rest of the group put their cups and spoons on one of these bags as well. The cooks also will need the large metal spoon, a large pot with lid, and hot pot tongs or grips.

The stove should be separate from the bags, and be fully fueled and ready to light. Extra gas should be kept away from the kitchen, preferably under the dining fly. Position the stove on a flat surface, such as the ground or a large, flat rock. When lighting the stove, stay in a crouched position so that you can step back if there's a flare-up. Never light the stove with your face over the burner, or with the stove placed between your legs. The crew members should all know how to light the stove, and have practiced lighting it before coming to Philmont.

Most crews use backpacking stoves that use white gas, which can be resupplied at backcountry commissary camps. Beginning in the 2008 season Philmont will be providing replacement iso-butane canisters, so crews no longer have to pack all the fuel for the whole trek. Note that iso-butane stoves may have too small a burner for the large aluminum pots provided by Philmont. Test the stove at home with an equivalent pot to make sure the system is compatible.

Before any food handling takes place, the cooks must wash their hands with soap and water or use hand sanitizer. The most common way that disease spread among crews is not washing hands, then touching food or dishes.

Boiling Water

Once the stove is lit, place a pot of water on the burner to boil. The meal will have directions on the packaging for the amount of water needed to hydrate the food. Estimate a little extra, as some of the water will evaporate from boiling. If you do not want to do the math, there is a way to estimate the amount of water needed. In each aluminum pot there is a wear line from constant use. Fill the pot to this line and add a little extra. Add treated water if more is needed after boiling.

Let the water boil with a lid covering the pot. This reduces boiling time. If using water from a stream or other non-purified source, the water must reach a rolling boil. This is when the water is bubbling violently, such as when boiling a pot of coffee. If utensils and pots need to be sterilized, then the water must be at a rolling boil, even if it's been treated.

Some people think that the water must be boiling for five minutes before use to kill any bugs. However, if the water has reached a rolling boil, it has been boiling for several minutes already, and has already reached the critical temperature at which nothing can live, and is clean.

Sterilization

Before dishes and utensils can be used for cooking or eating, they must be sterilized.

Unlike cooking, water for cleaning dishes does not have to be sterile. Also, after a day in the pack, they have been contaminated with dust, or may still have some soap residue from last night. Sterilization also ensures cleanliness, and reduces the chance of spreading bacteria or viruses.

To sterilize dishes, the water must be at a continuous rolling boil. If the stove is shut off, then the water temperature immediately goes down below that required to sanitize the dishes. Use hot pot tongs or grips to fully immerse the utensil or dish in the water. Hold it for a few seconds in the water before removing it. A good method for sterilizing dishes is to dip the bowls and cups first, setting them on a bear bag, then place the spoons in a clean dish after they have been sterilized. Placing spoons directly on the bear bags will contaminate them again.

Cooking

Before cooking food, open individual food pouches and bags by cutting near the top with a pocketknife. This can be done while waiting for water to boil. Pour contents into the pot, being careful to avoid spilling food particles onto the ground. One technique for cooking dinner is the one-pot method, with all food packages except for the dessert emptied into one pot and cooked. Keep the pot on the stove as heat will rehydrate food quickly. Stir the pot, making sure to scrape the bottom of the pot so that food does not burn on the bottom. Stir with one hand and hold the pot steady with hot pot tongs with the other hand to keep the pot steady.

After a few minutes lift the pot off the stove and place it on level ground. Occasionally stir the pot, and let the food rehydrate. If necessary, add water if the mixture is too thick or place the pot back on the stove to evaporate excess water so that the meal is less soupy.

Other methods for cooking dinner include cooking each part of the entrée separately. Still another method is hydrating certain parts of the meal, such as the peas or beef cubes separately in their foil packages with hot water. This allows these foods to hydrate, but not be mixed in with the whole meal. This could be important for people who prefer not to mix their food together, or for vegetarians who would not want to eat the dehydrated beef or chicken. Use whichever method works for the crew, the important thing is that everyone gets a hot meal in the evening.

When cooking the meal, the cooks or other crew members should be careful not to tip over the pot. Keep the stove and cook pot outside of high traffic areas in camp. No one should have to step across or over the pot. If the pot is tipped over, get as much food as possible back into the pot as quickly as possible. If a large amount of food is on the ground, the crew may have to eat the meal with a little dirt mixed in. If there is a relatively minor amount on the ground, it can be eaten or disposed in the garbage.

Before eating, it is a Philmont tradition to recite the Philmont grace.

Cleanup

Dishwashing is done after the meal is over. Water should be heated in the unused pot. The water does not have to be boiled, only heated. While the water is heating all of the used dishes can be placed on a bear bag, once the water is ready place the pot next to the bag. Pour half the water in the cook pot, then squirt a small amount of soap, no more than a drop, into the cook pot. Wash all dishes and utensils in this pot, and make sure to wash the cook pot and lid, if necessary. Dip these dishes in the rinse pot, then place them on the bear bag.

When all the dishes have been washed, it's time to sump the dishwater. The Philmont sumps are PVC pipes that go about three feet down into the ground, and extend out about twelve feet. This long section of tube is perforated with holes, and sits on a bed of gravel. The system acts much like a septic field. The water is poured down the sump, is drained into the gravel bed, and eventually percolates down to the water table. Most campsites have their own sump, although a few do share. The top of the sump with the metal screen has a rubber gasket that connects it to the main pipe. This is so that if a curious bear swipes the sump head while looking for food, the sump head will harmlessly pop off without damaging the main pipe.

A Philmont sump is used to drain grey water from cleanup. It helps to identify a campsite, and is also part of the Bearmuda Triangle.

Bring all the dishes on the bear bag to the sump, along with the pots, the sump strainer, rubber scraper, and a resealable plastic bag. Hold the strainer over the sump screen and pour the wash water from the cook pot into the sump. The strainer should catch the large food particles, while the metal screen on the sump catches the smaller particles. Once the cook pot is emptied, pour the rinse water into the cook pot, swish it around, then drain it down through the Frisbee.

Now take the rubber scraper and scrape off the food from the sump strainer into the plastic bag. These small bits of food are called "Yum-Yums" and the bag the "Yum-Yum Bag." Make sure to scrape the wire mesh with the rubber spatula for food particles.

If you are camping in an area without a sump, such as Valle Vidal, you will have to make one. Take an empty trail meal bag and fill it with pine needles and other "duff." Cut several holes in the bottom of the bag, enough so that water can drain through quickly. Once the dishes have been washed, carry them with the bag 200 feet away from your camp. Pour the grey water into the bag the same as if it ways a regular sump (see Chapter 8 on cooking and cleanup). The water will drain onto the ground, leaving food particles inside the bag. Store this bag in another resealable bag, and hang it in the bear bag. Leave the dishes by your sump.

Some Rangers teach to pour the dishwater onto a pile of rocks to concentrate the smell. Before leaving camp the next day, toss the rocks in different directions far away from camp to disperse the impact.

Take all the dishes and place them in the two pots by the sump, and cover with lids. This is called "bombproofing" and it serves two purposes. One, it keeps smaller rodents from scurrying around in your dishes. Second, if a bear knocks over the pots during the night, they act like a burglar alarm. The pots always stay by the sump, as they are considered smellables. However, since, they do not have foodstuffs on them, they are not considered *rewardables*. More on this subject later.

The bear bags, sump strainer, rubber scraper, and Yum-Yum bag all go up with the bear bags in the evening.

Here's an idea for evening cleanup. While the dishwater is heating up after dinner, the rest of the crew can brush their teeth at the sump. Toothpaste is to be spit down the screen, but usually there is a big blob on the screen. The toothpaste will be forced down the sump when pouring the dishwater. By doing this the crew does not have to waste purified water to clean the sump head.

If your crew decides to have dessert, there are many tasty options provided in the trail meals. These treats often require no heating, and can be rehydrated in their pouches, making cleanup easier. For the first night on the trail the Ranger packs a special treat for the crew.

Remember

1. Philmont meals provide about 3,000 calories a day.
2. Trail meals are a mix of carbohydrates and protein.
3. Organize trail meals into piles for meal selection.
4. Designate a kitchen area, light the stove, and wash your hands!
5. Sterilize all cookware in water that is at a roiling boil.
6. Cook food over heat, remember to stir.
7. Clean dishes with one drop of soap.

8. Drain all dishwater down the sump.
9. Empty bear bags, sump strainer, rubber scraper, scrubbie pad, and Yum-Yum bag get hung in the bear bags.

Chapter 9: Bears and Mountain Lions

VIEWING WILDLIFE CAN BE A FUN and exhilarating experience, but there are precautions your crew must take to be safe, especially with bears and mountain lions.

Black Bears

There are approximately 250 black bears, *ursus americanus* on Philmont. That is one bear for every square mile, although their ranges extend much farther, and overlap with other private properties bordering Philmont as well as the Carson National Forest and Eliot Barker Wildlife Area. They can grow up to six feet long and three feet high, and vary in size from less than 150 lbs to almost 500 lbs. Their fur can be black, but also brown cinnamon, or yellow, with a white patch of fur on the chest. Black bears also have a "Roman Nose" facial profile, with their snouts extending far out from the face.

Black bears are the only species of bear in New Mexico and Philmont. At one time grizzly bears did exist in the area, but were hunted to extinction by the 20th century. They are now found from Wyoming north to Alaska.

The bears at Philmont enjoy a variety of natural foods, which include nuts, berries, insects, grubs, and carrion, dead meat that has been killed already. The majority of their food comes from plant sources, with approximately ten percent of the bears' diet consisting of carrion. These bears are opportunistic animals, looking for as much food as they can find to build up enough body fat to hibernate. Thus, the majority of the time they are awake during the summer is spent eating.

Bear Procedures on the Trail

It is possible that your crew may encounter a black bear while hiking. A common misconception is that if you see a bear you should, "play dead." This technique is more appropriate for grizzlies. Remember, black bears are scavengers that like to eat the carcasses of other animals. However, they rarely hunt their own food. If a bear is spotted from far away, such as the opposite end of the meadow at Lover's Leap Camp, the bear may not have seen you. The crew should stay quiet, maybe even take some non-flash pictures, and back away slowly. Let the bear have its space, and eventually, it will move along.

A crew can be so focused on hiking that it will oftentimes surprise a bear when turning a corner in the trail. When this happens the crew needs to gather together quickly in a tight group, shout loudly and make noise, and back away slowly. The bear should become frightened, and will either run away or run up a tree. However, the bear may decide to bluff charge the crew, veering away before making contact. It is testing you to see if you are a threat. This can be a scary situation, but the crew must hold its ground and not run. Running tells the bear that you are food, and it will chase you. Do not try to climb a tree to escape, as black bears are excellent climbers. Staying together and making lots of noise is the best defense.

Be especially careful if you encounter a bear with cubs. Bears can be protective of newborn young, and a mother will defend its cubs if it believes there is a threat. Do not get in between a mother and her cubs, nor try to alert a bear of your presence. Give them as much space as possible.

If you are attacked by a black bear, fight for your life. Try to hit it in the nose, which is very sensitive. Don't play dead. A black bear is very strong, with powerful paws and teeth that can rip apart meat. They are also very timid animals who do not normally hunt live prey. If the bear is attacking you, then it is a desperate situation.

Bears in Camp

It is not uncommon for bears to wander into camps, either because they are curious or because they are looking for food. Bears are intelligent animals, and quickly learn where they can find food.

If your crew does see a bear in camp, the procedure is similar to seeing a bear on the trail. Gather your group together, make lots of noise, and try to make yourselves look bigger. If the bear continues towards you, the crew should back away very slowly as a group, continuing to make noise. Be concerned if the bear does not run away, or ignores your calls, as these are signs that the bear has become accustomed to people, and has most likely had a taste of human food. If necessary, abandon your camp to the bear and give it a wide berth. It is much easier to replace a torn pack than it is to replace a person.

What if I Hear Something at Night?

Bears are active during the evening hours. If someone hears a noise outside the tent, they should wake up their tent-mate. Start talking in low voices and wake up the other crew members. With everyone talking in low voices, the bear will realize that something is not right, and will walk away. Do not yell or scream, this will startle the bear, and may cause it to be violent. If there are no more sounds after a few minutes, then it is okay to go back to sleep.

What About My Inhaler?

Medications are smellables too, and must go up in the bear bag. But some crew members need an inhaler or epi-pen handy for emergencies. These items can be kept down at night in a dirty sock, stored in one's boots. The boots should be kept in the tent, not only to keep them dry, but also because insects, scorpions, or small snakes may try to make a home inside.

Prevention

Keeping a smellables-free camp is the best way to prevent a bear from entering your campsite. It takes someone with a trained eye and who is a bit obsessive-compulsive, but it can be done.

The highest concentration of smellables will be in the Bearmuda Triangle. Always double-check that all food scraps and trash have been policed up from the fire ring and sump. Everyone should have his eye out for any wrappers or scraps of food lying on the ground.

Before raising the bear bags in the evening, have everyone check their backpacks and pockets for food, trash, lip balm, etc. Scouts always seem to forget about those small items, especially if the crew is rushed to hang the bags. They should have their personal ditty bags in the bear bags, as well as any water bottles *that have ever had drink mix in them.* All other water bottles should be kept in the fire ring. Do not bring water bottles into tents or leave them lying out overnight, as a bear may recognize the bottle as a food source. If there are leftovers from dinner, or pots that could not be cleaned, hang these items in the bear bag until they are disposed of or cleaned.

Always double-check that everything necessary is up in the bear bags. Sometimes Scouts will cut corners by stuffing an empty drink mix package under a rock, "Out of site, out of mind." This is not acceptable, as the bear can easily smell the wrapper. Scouts have also been known to throw unwanted food down the latrine, thinking that the odor will mask the food smell. This is also incorrect, and instead of simply having a habituated bear, you'll have a habituated bear with poop all over its face, as well as a destroyed latrine!

If the clothing you are wearing has food stains, remove the clothing and store it overnight in the bear bags. Washing the clothing the next day will remove the food odor. At night, after the bags have been hung, change out of your day clothes into sleep clothes before bedtime. Store your day clothes in your pack. The clothes you were wearing during the day will have salt stains, suntan lotion residue, and may have absorbed food odor from cooking dinner. This is why you should bring gym shorts and a t-shirt for sleep clothes, as you can still walk around camp while still decent.

When all is said and done, all that should be left in camp after the bear bags are hung are packs with covers on, leaning against trees near or under the dining fly, with water bottles, stoves, and fuel bottles in the fire ring. The black trash bags, camp shovel, and toilet paper should be under the dining fly. Pots, dishes, and utensils, are left at sump.

Bill Sassani

The Smellables Police

Despite all the information and training Philmont provides participants, there are numerous bear violations every night across Philmont, especially after the Ranger leaves the crew on day 3. To reinforce bear policies, Philmont staff will police campsites and issue citations if necessary, either directly to the crew or taped to one of the dining fly poles if no one's around. Campsite checks are conducted by Backcountry staff, Rangers, and the Bear Researchers. If no one is in camp, and smellables are found on the ground, these items may be collected by staff and left at the staff cabin, if in a staffed camp, or hung in a bear bag at a bear cable. This can be frustrating for crews, but it is meant to be in the crews' best interest and safety.

Mountain Lions

Mountain Lions, *felis concolor*, at Philmont are about five feet long and weigh between 120–200 lbs. They are tan in color, and have a black-tipped tail that can extend up to three feet from the body. They are carnivores that eat large animals such as elk and deer, as well as smaller creatures such as porcupines, mice, skunks, and rabbits.

The procedures for bear encounters on the trail are the same for mountain lions. It is very rare to actually see a mountain lion, since most of the time they will run away if they hear humans. Some have described hearing a mountain lion call as a shriek or scream, and there have been rare instances of people being watched or stalked by mountain lions. If you do see one, be sure the crew stays together and makes noise. Also avoid walking by yourself in the evening when in camp, especially in the North and Middle Ponil areas and Abreu.

Reporting Sightings

All bear and mountain lion sightings should be reported to the nearest staff camp. When making the report, note where you saw the animal, what was it doing, whether it got into human food or trash, whether it had ear tags and how many, and whether it displayed any behavior that was either aggressive towards humans or ignored humans.

Philmont's procedures for bears can seem so specific and detailed that it seems to be overly cautious. But they are necessary not only to protect humans, but also the bears themselves. Each summer several bears are relocated, and one or two must be destroyed when they have returned to their old habits. Deliberately feeding a bear is illegal under New Mexico state law. As visitors to Philmont it is our duty to protect these animals so that future Scouts can enjoy them.

Remember

1. Black bears are part of Philmont's habitat, eating plants, insects, and carrion.
2. If you see a bear, get in a group, make lots of noise, and make yourselves look big.
3. If your hear something at night, make soft conversation.
4. Store inhalers and epi-pens in a dirty sock in your boot at night.
5. Police your campsite and each other for smellables.
6. Staff do campsite checks regularly.
7. Mountain lion procedures are the same for bears.
8. Report bear and mountain lion sightings to the nearest staff camp.

Chapter 10: Water Purification and Hygiene

WATER IS A CRUCIAL and precious resource in the Southwest, and this is certainly true at Philmont. A Scout that is participating in strenuous physical activity, such as hiking, must drink six to eight quarts of water a day to maintain proper hydration. This amount is more than what most people are accustomed to drinking, especially if they are not from the Southwest, where the air is drier, the elevation is higher, and the sun is more intense. Moisture from the body evaporates at a faster rate, even when one is resting. Moreover, it even may be lost during exercise with less apparent perspiration. Not drinking enough water can cause dehydration and contribute to more serious health concerns.

Because maintaining fluid intake is so important, Philmont has several systems in place to ensure participants have enough water to drink, as well as to stay clean and to maintain proper hygiene while in the backcountry. Using these systems are important to prevent illness, and to avoid the possibly of being evacuated to Base Camp.

Bill Sassani

What's in the Water?

Giardia is a protozoa commonly found in streams, ponds, and lakes on Philmont. Giardia is disseminated by animal effluent, from both wildlife and commercial livestock, getting into streams and creeks. If this water is consumed without purification, the organism will take root in the digestive system, causing violent diarrhea. To reinforce this to my crews, I say that Giardia causes, "violent, uncontrollable, frothy, green, foamy diarrhea!" If contracted while on the trail, the unsuspecting camper may not realize that he/she has it until after the trek, as it takes about two weeks for illness to appear.

The only way to prevent getting sick is to purify your water before drinking it. Forget the idealized notion of drinking from a fresh, clear-running mountain stream. Those days are long gone.

Chlorinated Water

Philmont provides purified water at most staff camps. This is done by a pumping and chlorination system that runs on solar power. These systems pump water from a well, then send the water through an injector system that adds chlorine at regular intervals. The water is then stored in a holding tank, usually on a hill above the camp, and is gravity-fed to faucets. The water is checked daily by the camp staff members, who measure the amount of chlorine coming out of the faucet. It is a simple system that works amazingly well.

Some staff camps provide just chlorinated water, while others have showers as well. There are three staff camps that do not provide treated water, and require the crews to use their own purification systems. These are Black Mountain, Crooked Creek, and French Henry. These camps are either too remote to maintain a system or do not have an adequate aquifer to support the staff and crew. However, there are streams that run through these camps that have reliable flow rates. Review your itinerary before hitting the trail so that you know when you will be staying at these camps during your trek.

Micropur Tablets

Micropur tablets were introduced during the summer of 2006 as a means to purify water, and are the primary method for crews to treat unpurified water. They are lightweight, easy to use chlorine dioxide tablets, and are effective in killing all organisms in water. To use Micropur, tear open a single pouch, being careful not to let the tablet touch your fingers. Empty the pouch into an open bottle of water, and close the cap. You should see the tablet begin to dissolve, creating a stream of bubbles. Allow five minutes for the tablet to dissolve in the water. One tablet purifies one quart of water.

Once the tablet is dissolved, turn the water bottle upside down and loosen the cap until a trickle of water comes out. This is called "bleeding the threads," and its purpose is to clean off the threads of the cap and bottle. It defeats the purpose of cleaning the water inside the bottle if the water on the threads is still dirty from when you dipped it in the stream or pond.

Allow thirty minutes for the chlorine to take effect before consuming. During this time do add drink mixes into the bottle, as this will counteract the chlorine. If the water is 0 degrees C, allow up to two hours for the chlorine to take full effect.

There are a few drawbacks to Micropur. The product has a short shelf-life, and is effective for only one season. The tablets can be corrosive, so avoid direct contact with the skin.

Your crew will be issued several sleeves of Micropur at Base Camp. Additional supplies can be picked up at the backcountry commissary camps.

Water Filters

Backpacking water filters are easily available these days and work very well to filter out water-borne protozoa. They work by sucking water from a stream or pond and squeezing the water through a filter, which catches the contaminants and drains the water into a container. Many filters come with pre-filters to screen out large particulates, iodine cartridges to kill bacteria, and charcoal filters to filter out the iodine taste.

Philmont recommends that crews carry a filter, in addition to Micropur. Filters are required for attending the Double H High Adventure Base. Know how to use your filter, and have adequate supplies of replacement cartridges and spare parts. Also buy enough filters to provide enough water for the whole crew, one may not be enough. When buying a filter, determine what it removes, how it operates, and how easy it is to use and service in the field. Ask the store clerk if you can test one before buying it.

Getting This Stuff

Micropur, Polar Pure, and water filters all can be found at local backpacking shops and major outdoor retailers. The Philmont trading post, Tooth of Time Traders, sells Micropur and water filters on its website: www.toothoftimetraders.com. Micropur will be issued to the crew as part of the crew equipment at Services. It is a good idea to buy these systems ahead of time and practice their use at home on a shakedown hike.

Boiling

Boiling water is an acceptable way of ensuring that it is safe to drink. The water must have reached a rolling boil to be drinkable. Boiled water that is drunk after it has been cooled can have an unpleasant taste. Adding drink mix can solve this problem, or, use the hot water to make tea, coffee or other warm drinks.

Hygiene

Staying clean in the backcountry is an important factor in having a successful trek. Granted, everyone is going to get dirty, smelly, and have sweat stains on pack straps and t-shirts. But there are a few things the crew can do to maintain hygiene and prevent illness.

The simplest thing you can do is wash your hands. By washing hands after using the latrine and before eating, the crew can cut down the potential spread of bacteria and illness. Use an alcohol-based hand sanitizer when soap and water is not available.

Bathing regularly is another useful method of staying clean. There will be several opportunities during the trek for the crew members to shower. Take advantage of this resource, and encourage your crew to shower.

When showers are not available, such as at trail camps, one can take a bandanna bath. Take a water bottle with purified water, the liquid trail soap, and a bandanna to a private spot away from others. Wet the bandanna and use a sparing amount of soap to wash vital areas and rinse. Rinsing the dirt off the legs arms, and face can also be refreshing. An alternative to bandanna baths are using large, moistened towellettes.

Make sure to include foot maintenance as part of your daily routine. Give your feet time to air out during the day, and check for blisters and hot spots. Rinse your feet with clean water and let them air dry, then rub

your fingers in between the toes to get rid of
the toe-jam. Change socks frequently.

Laundry can be done at staff camps with
showers, which provide large sinks, wash
tubs, and scrubbers. If in a trail camp, a t-
shirt or a pair of socks can be washed in a
resealable plastic bag using cold water and a
drop of soap. Make sure to drain the wash
water down the sump. Be careful about using clotheslines to dry laundry, as they often
get left up overnight and people may get
caught in them, causing injury to the neck or
face. A good method for drying clothes is to
spread them out on the dining fly. Air drying,
plus the sun and warm nylon will dry the
clothes faster.

Dry Camps

There are several backcountry trail
camps that are considered dry camps where
no water is available, whether treated or un-
treated. Mount Phillips and Tooth Ridge
Camp are examples. When staying at these
camps crews must top off all water bottles
and crew water containers at the prior staff
camp or available water source. Refer to the
cooking chapter for tricks on cooking without
water and saving weight.

In the Valle Vidal, there are water
sources available for crews to get water, then
treat. Crews traveling in this area can get
water out of McCrystal Creek, the stream in
Seally Canyon, and other streams or ponds.
Whiteman Vega has a stock tank that runs
regularly, and the camp provides a washba-

sin and scrub board to wash clothes. Make sure to wash clothes away from the tank so as not to get soap in it, as cattle and horses also use the water for drinking.

Logistics maintains a bulletin board which lists the availability of water in each backcountry camp. Check this board before leaving for the trail.

The Scouts may resist taking showers, after all, "Dirt don't hurt," right? Others may dislike drinking the water, even with drink mix, as some of the backcountry camps have methane in the water table. Ponil is famous for its gassy water. Remind them that the mark of a true outdoors person is more than hiking lots of miles and carrying heavy loads, but someone who can take care of himself and stay healthy. After all, "A Scout is clean."

Remember:

1. Purify water to kill Giardia.
2. Most staff camps provide chlorinated water.
3. Mircopur, water filters, and boiling can be used to purify water from un-treated sources.
4. Wash hands and bathe regularly to prevent transmission of disease or in-fections.
5. Some trail camps are dry, and require packing in water.
6. Staying clean is part of the Scout Law!

Medical Concerns and Emergencies

Injuries frequently occur in the Philmont backcountry. Most of these injuries are relatively minor, requiring only an alcohol pad and a bandage. Some injuries though are so serious that they require treatment, and potentially, evacuation. This chapter reviews the most common injuries that occur to participants on a trek and how to treat them. Chapter 13 discusses other safety issues at Philmont and how to report an emergency.

Chapter 11: First Aid

THERE ARE NINETEEN first aid topics taught by the Philmont Rangers. Below is an overview of each problem and possible treatment. However, what is covered here does not rule out all potential medical situations that could occur in the backcountry, and should not be considered "the Gospel." To better understand backcountry medical issues and treatment, consider getting trained from a reputable wilderness medicine company. Philmont requires that at least one person in the crew has gone through a 16-hour Wilderness First Aid course, and that one person has been certified in CPR.

Dehydration

Dehydration is the most common ailment for participants, and it is the most preventable. Dehydration occurs from not drinking enough water, at least six to eight quarts a day. Symptoms include headache, dizziness, irritability, chapped lips, dry skin, nosebleeds, and altered mental state. A good benchmark to determine hydration is urine output. If there is not much urine, and if it is yellow or darker, then you must drink more water. If there is a lot of urine and it is clear, then you are hydrated. Rangers call this being "clear and copious."

To prevent dehydration, drink water frequently throughout the day. Hydration systems with a bladder and drinking tube allow the user to drink water in small sips without having to stop. Before a hike, crew members will raise their water bottles in a toast. Discourage the crew from chugging water, as it will pass through the body and not be absorbed into tissue. Drinking an excessive amount of water too quickly can cause hyponatremia, a potentially fatal condition where there is too little sodium in the body. Also discourage the crew from drinking large amounts of caffeinated beverages such as coffee, tea, or soda. They actually can make you more dehydrated by encouraging urination. Avoid using rehydration salts, as there is plenty of sodium in the drink mixes and the food provided by Philmont.

Dehydration is often a contributing factor for other injuries or illnesses. For instance, a Scout who has not been drinking water stumbles over a tree root, spraining his ankle. Now you have two problems to deal with. Also, if one is not properly hydrated it could lead to heat exhaustion.

Heat Exhaustion

Heat exhaustion is caused by exposure to the sun, warm temperatures, and dehydration. Hiking for a long time, especially during the afternoon, causes the body's temperature to rise. The body combats this by producing sweat. Someone with heat exhaustion will be very sweaty with cool and clammy skin, tired and irritable, and will have a rapid pulse.

Treat the patient by getting him into the shade and drinking water. Add some drink mix for taste to encourage drinking. Have the patient keep drinking until he/she is Clear and Copious. If heat exhaustion is not treated, it could lead to heat stroke.

Heat Stroke

The body's temperature is so high, 104 degrees, that the patient is in danger of having a stroke. The patient will have dry, warm skin as the body has stopped sweating. The patient may be delirious, and could become unconscious and possibly die.

Time is critical for treating heat stroke. Get the patient into the shade and onto a pad. Remove clothing to allow heat to escape. Wet bandannas and spread them onto the patient to cool the skin and to lower the body temperature. Use a folded foam pad to fan the patient. Do not immerse the patient into a creek. Fast changes in temperature could cause the patient to go into shock. Have the patient drink water if he/she is conscious and able to swallow. Do not force water down the throat of an unconscious patient. Notify staff, as the patient must be evacuated to Base Camp for treatment.

Heat stroke, like heat exhaustion and dehydration, can be avoided by drinking water, taking rest breaks, and avoiding hiking in the afternoon heat, when the sun's rays are most intense.

Hypothermia

Hypothermia can occur when the temperature drops and there is rain or snow. Patients may start shivering and have pale, cold skin. The condition can become more serious if the patient becomes incoherent, loses fine motor coordination such as the ability to button a shirt, and may slip into unconscious. A patient can die from hypothermia.

Treat a hypothermic patient by removing the cold environment. This can include changing into dry clothes, and/or slipping the patient into a sleeping bag in a tent. If possible, get the patient into a staff cabin and sit them next to the stove. Provide warm drinks and high energy snacks if the patient is conscious and able to swallow. Place warm (but not hot) insulated water bottles under the armpits and in the groin area to promote heat. If the patient is unconscious monitor his breathing. Do not get into a sleeping bag with a patient, as your body heat will be drained away by the patient, leaving you cold. Instead, keep the patient in the sleeping bag, but have people in a tent with the patient. Their ambient body heat will raise the air temperature, and their companionship will be a comfort to the patient.

Prevent hypothermia by constantly eating snacks and drinking water to maintain energy. Dress in layers with synthetic clothing that will keep you warm even when wet. Have sturdy rainwear that will keep out moisture but allow sweat from the body to escape. Avoid wearing cotton garments, such as t-shirts and jeans. Monitor the crew, especially when it is cold and wet, for signs of hypothermia. If one person is cold, then most likely the rest of the crew is cold as well.

Sunburn

With low humidity and high elevations, the ultraviolet radiation produced by the sun can easily cause a sunburn. Areas that are most likely to burn are the tips of the ears, nose and face, and the back of the neck.

Treat sunburned areas by cooling the skin with purified water and cover with clothing. If there is a blister, do not pop it, as it will then be open to infection. Treat any popped blisters by keeping the area clean and covered.

Prevention includes wearing hats that shield the face and neck, and applying sunscreen in the morning before hiking, and reapplying throughout the day. Do not apply sunscreen after 5 PM, as it may not wear off before bedtime, and could attract bears. Discourage Scouts from wearing sleeveless shirts or going without a shirt, as sunburns on the shoulders can be very uncomfortable, plus it can make it impossible to carry a backpack.

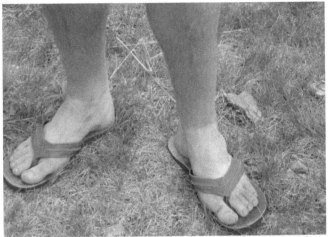

An example of a severe sunburn. Even in black-and-white, the difference between the burned and unburned skin is clearly visible.

If the sunburn is very large, it may require evacuation to Base Camp. More on determining burn size below.

Burns

Burns are caused by external sources such as heat, chemical, electrical, or radiation. There are three kinds of burns: superficial, partial-thickness, and full-thickness. Superficial burns appear as a sunburn, with reddened, swollen skin. Partial-thickness burns have blisters which can be very painful. Full-thickness burns have charred skin down to the deeper tissue. There will be little pain at the burn area as nerves have been destroyed. However, full-thickness burns will be surrounded with partial-thickness and superficial burns, which will be quite painful.

To treat a burn, first remove the heat source, such as moving away from a fire. Carefully remove clothing and jewelry, but leave any that has bonded with flesh. Assess the extent of injury, and cool the burn with purified water. Apply a cool, non-stick dressing to the burn, and keep the area clean.

If a burn is greater than 5% of the body, the patient must be evacuated. The size of the palm of your hand is approximately 1% of the body, so use this as a guide when determining how big the burn is. Full-thickness burns must be evacuated no matter how big it is. Evacuate a patient if there are burns on the shoulders, face, or genital areas.

To prevent burns, use caution when operating stoves, handling pots of hot water, or when walking around campfires. There have been numerous instances where Scouts have been burned when they accidentally kicked over a hot pot of water because they were not paying attention to what they were doing, or were walking in the designated cooking area, with the hot water pouring down the boot. If this occurs, pour cold water into the boot to cool the burn before removing the boot and assessing the injury.

Altitude Sickness

Altitude sickness is caused by ascending too quickly before the body can adjust. In its initial stages it has been described as feeling lethargic, ill, and having a lack of appetite.

Patients may also have increased heart and respiratory rates. I tell my crews that you just feel awful and that you don't want to do anything. Occasionally, it may progress to headache and even pulmonary (lung) and cerebral (brain) edema. The only way to treat altitude sickness is to descend to a lower altitude. Anyone exhibiting more severe symptoms must be evacuated to a lower altitude immediately.

There is nothing one can do to prevent altitude sickness. It can affect someone who is in top physical condition as well as the couch potato. Philmont does design its treks to allow time to acclimate by having crews stay their first night at Philmont in Base Camp, at 6,000 feet. The second and third nights are spent at progressively higher elevations, both of which are below 9,000 feet. Spending a few days sightseeing in New Mexico or Colorado, which have higher altitudes than in other areas of the United States, before arriving at Philmont can aid in acclimation process.

Snake/Rodent Bites

Western diamondback rattlesnakes are common at Philmont, especially in areas surrounding Ponil, Indian Writings, Rayado River Camp, and Abreu. Although it rarely happens, people may be bitten by snakes when they are walking down the trail and are not paying attention. Often, it's not the first person that is bitten, but the second or third person in line. The snake will bite just above the ankle, leaving two puncture marks. Adult snakes do not always inject venom, especially if they bite an animal larger than the snake. Young snakes have not yet learned to control their venom, and may inject all their venom into a victim.

If bitten by a snake, first remember to get the patient away from the snake in order to administer treatment. Keep the bite area clean by washing it with purified water, keep the patient from moving too much, remove constricting items such as watches and rings, and treat for shock. Identify the snake, but do not try to kill the animal. It's not worth risking another person getting bitten. Notify the nearest staff camp, as the patient must be evacuated to Base Camp. Do not try to suck the venom out of the wound with your mouth, which has been popularized in movies. This method is unsanitary for both the patient and the rescuer, and is a way to spread blood-borne diseases.

The procedure for rodent bites is the same for snakebite. The concern with rodents is contracting rabies. To prevent snake and rodent bites, watch where you are walking and avoid handling squirrels or mice.

A rattlesnake slither's away. Be aware of where you walk in camp and on the trail to avoid stepping on one and being bitten.

Severe Bleeding

Severe bleeding is caused by deep cuts. To stop the bleeding, apply direct pressure with a dressing while wearing latex gloves. Elevate the area above the heart. Clean the wound with soap and warm water, or irrigate using cold purified water and a syringe or a resealable plastic bag with a hole in the corner. Cleaning the wound removes dirt that could cause an infection. Cover with a gauze pad or clear wound pad with antibiotic ointment. Pads are now made that are thin plastic sheets that cover the wound and keep it dry. It can be worn for several days without needing to change it.

If it is a severe wound, report it at the next staff camp for additional treatment. If it requires stitches the patient may be sent to the Health Lodge. You can prevent serious cuts by practicing knife safety.

Stopped Breathing

For stopped breathing administer CPR to the patient until relieved by someone of higher medical training or completely exhausted. Have someone contact the nearest staff camp immediately.

Hyperventilation

Strenuous hiking in thin air can easily cause someone to hyperventilate. A crew member suffering from hyperventilation will be conscious and show obvious distress, exhaling rapidly. For treatment, make eye contact with the patient, and speak calmly. Tell the patient to relax and to mimic your breathing. Inhale and exhale slowly, making sure the patient is following your lead. If the patient passes out, monitor him to make sure he is breathing.

The Pacesetter can prevent hyperventilation by keeping a pace that everyone can handle and still be able to talk to other crew members comfortably without sounding winded.

Heart Attack

Heart attacks are caused by inadequate circulation to the heart muscle, and are usually precipitated by exercise. Symptoms can include shortness of breath, feeling tired, tingling in the left arm, pain radiating to the arm or jaw, nausea and vomiting. The skin may feel pale, cool, and sweaty. Pulse can be rapid, slow, and weak. The patient may complain of the feeling of a heavy weight on the chest. Be concerned if the patient has a prior history of heart problems.

Treat a heart attack patient by making him comfortable. Have him lie on a pad in the shade and loosen clothing. Monitor his condition and encourage sipping water in small amounts. If the patient is already taking heart medication, administer it, or, the patient can take half of an adult aspirin tablet in order to prevent blood clotting. Contact the nearest staff camp immediately for evacuation.

Blisters/Foot Care

Blisters and hot spots are caused when the foot rubs against the sock and boot, creating a friction burn. Signs of a hot spot are red skin and tenderness, while a blister will have puffy skin filled with fluid. Common blister spots on the foot include the outsides of the big toe and pinky toe, the front of the toes, the ball of the heel, and the back of the heel.

If you find a hot spot, cover the area with a band aid and monitor for blister development. If a blister develops, use moleskin or mole foam to protect the blister and to pad it. Cut a "doughnut" hole in the padding big enough to surround the blister. Cover with a band aid and medical tape. Make sure to check the blister regularly and keep the area clean.

The blister may pop on its own, causing the fluid to drain. This creates an open wound that is susceptible to infection. Monitor the blister and keep the area clean, airing it out when you have the opportunity. Frequently change the bandage and wear clean socks. For easier maintenance, use bandages which seal out air and keep the blister clean. Avoid popping blisters in the field if you can.

Prevent blisters and hot spots from forming with regular foot checks. Wash your feet to get rid of dirt and toe-jam, which can build up after a day of hiking on dusty trails. Some participants wear ankle gaiters to keep the dirt out of their boots. Having footwear that fits properly and is well broken-in is also important.

Broken Bones

There are several ways to break a bone at Philmont, such as slipping and falling while hiking, falling off a horse, or even just stepping on an uneven surface. The patient will feel pain at the affected area, and there may be a deformity. The patient may not be able to use the limb, or may have limited range. The skin will be swollen and purplish. In a severe compound fracture the bone will be protruding through the skin with bleeding.

To treat a broken bone, you must first determine the extent of the damage. Remove clothing so you can see the injury. Look for skin discoloration, swelling, and deformity in the limb. Assess circulation, range of motion, and sensation in the limb. Immobilize the limb above and below the injury site. Surround the limb with padded objects, such as stuff sacks filled with dirt or logs covered with foam pads. Do not try to splint the injury, as Philmont medics will remove the splint to apply their own. Send runners to the nearest staff camp so that the Health Lodge can be contacted. The patient will need to be evacuated.

Sprains

It is easy to roll an ankle on the trail. Participants sometimes fail to pay attention when hiking, resulting in tripping over rocks, or someone plants his foot the wrong way in a game of ultimate Frisbee. A sprained ankle will be swollen, sore, and painful. There also may be limited range of motion in the ankle. The patient may not be able to bear weight on the affected limb.

Treat the sprain by applying RICE: Rest, Ice, Compression, and Elevation. Have the patient sit on a foam pad with the foot elevated, resting on a pack or sleeping bag. It is tough to find ice in the backcountry, but water from a stream and sealed in a resealable bag will work well. Apply the bag to the area and keep it in place with an elastic wrap or a bandanna tied around it. Keep the ice on 20–40 minutes in an hour to allow circulation in the foot.

Some find it possible to hike on to camp, but walking on an unsuspected fracture may worsen the injury. Be careful, take precautions by lightening the pack load, use trekking poles for stability, and watch where you step.

Prevent sprains by being aware of where you step. Trekking poles really to do work to relieve the weight on your legs and back, and help keep you stable, especially where the trail is rough or nonexistent.

Eye Injury

Common eye injuries include when a speck of dust gets into the eye, which can be solved by flushing the eye with purified water. More serious injuries are less common, but can result in impaling an eye with an object such as a tree branch.

The goal of treatment is to prevent further injury by avoiding pressure on the eye, keeping it clean, and preventing eye movement. Protection for the injured eye can be made by cutting the lower portion of a paper cup and taping it over the eye, being careful to make it large enough to rest on the bones around the eye socket rather than the eyelids. The other eye should be covered to discourage the patient from looking around. This is because the eyes work together, where one eye goes the other follows.

The patient will be upset and disoriented, so make sure there is someone next to the patient to keep him company and to keep the patient informed as to what is going on around them. Keep the patient still and send runners to the nearest staff camp.

Prevent eye injuries by being careful when around low tree limbs, especially at night.

Shock

Someone can go into shock either by suffering from a loss of blood or from witnessing someone else's medical injury. Someone in shock will have an irregular pulse, either rapid or weak, as well as irregular breathing. The skin will be pale, cool, and clammy. The patient will feel anxious, and may be nauseated.

Treat for shock by making the patient comfortable by lying on a pad with the feet elevated. Encourage the patient to drink water and keep him warm. For volume shock treat source of the bleeding.

Bee/Insect Stings

If someone in the crew is stung by a bee or an insect, monitor the area for swelling. Check with the patient to determine if he has been stung in the past, and whether or not he is allergic to beestings. The patient might experience mild swelling at the sting area, which can be treated with a Benadryl tablet. Some patients may go into anaphylactic shock quickly, a potentially fatal condition if not treated quickly.

If the patient has an epi-pen, use it immediately by injecting it in the top of the arm muscle. Monitor the patient carefully, additional doses may need to be administered. Immediately send runners to the nearest staff camp. All backcountry staff camps have epinephrine, or "epi"-pens in their first aid kits.

Remove stingers by using something with a stiff edge, such as a Philmont backpack tag card to gently scrape the stinger out of the skin. Do not use tweezers, as these will squeeze venom from the stinger into the skin. Wash the affected area with soap and water.

Make sure you know whether any of the participants in the crew are allergic to bee stings and carry epi-pens. These should be carried on the person at all times, and be easily accessible to the rest of the crew. Everyone should know where the epi-pen is kept. At night, epi-pens stay in a dirty sock in the camper's boot in his tent. Carry two epi-pens as a precaution in case more epi is needed.

Inhalers

The techniques for carrying an inhaler are the same as with epi-pens. Everyone in the crew should know where the inhaler is kept, and the participant should carry it with him at all times. At night the inhaler is stored on the ground in a dirty sock in the participants' boot inside their tent. Carry a backup inhaler.

The above descriptions are a brief overview of common medical injuries that may occur on a trek, and are not a complete list. For more information about medical concerns in the backcountry, refer to *Wilderness Medicine*, published by the National Outdoor Leadership School (NOLS). It is an excellent resource that describes different medical problems and treatment that might be performed in a backcountry setting,

Remember

1. The most common medical problem in the backcountry is dehydration. Drink 6–8 quarts a day to maintain adequate fluid intake.
2. Potential illnesses and injuries include, but are not limited to: heat exhaustion, heat stroke, hypothermia, sunburn, altitude sickness, snake/rodent bites, severe bleeding, stopped breathing, hyperventilation, heart attack, blisters, broken bones, sprains, burns, eye injury, shock, bee/insect stings.
3. Know how to use epi-pens and inhalers, and know where they are stored. Keep them with the participant at all times, even at night.
4. Expand your knowledge of backcountry medicine.

Chapter 12: Emergencies, Reporting Procedures, and Training

THERE ARE OTHER KINDS of emergencies that require a response from the crew. This chapter will review these other emergencies as well as how to report these incidents.

Reporting an Emergency

Emergency Procedures are referred to by Phimont as the method used to document an emergency and to transmit that information to the Health Lodge or Base Camp. These procedures are taught by the Ranger during a crew's first days at camp, and are copied by the Crew Leader onto the crew's map for easy reference.

When reporting a medical emergency, the following information should be written down:

- Name of the patient and initials.
- Age, birthdate, weight, gender.
- Expedition number and itinerary number.
- Location:
  - If in a trail camp, the site number.
  - If on the trail, grid coordinates.
- Time of the incident.

- Events leading up to the ill-ness/injury.
- Description of illness/injury. Symptoms.
- Pain: Severity on a scale of 0–10. Does it radiate, come and go, move, etc.?
- Vitals: pulse, respiratory rate, temperature, skin color/texture.
- Level of Conciousness
- Alert and Oriented x 4: Name, Time, Place, Incident
- Verbal
- Unresponsive
- History of present illness
- Treatment given so far.

Also include a SAMPLE history. This is:

- Signs/Symptoms
- Medications
- Past medical history.
- Last food/drink and last urination/bowel movement.
- Events leading up to the injury/illness.

Once all of the information has been documented, the crew should send four calm people to the nearest staff camp. These crew members should be able to hike quickly, but they need to stay together and to not go so fast as to not be safe. It is possible for the runners to injure themselves while trying to get help. Philmont thus requires four people to get help, in case someone gets hurt, one person can stay with the second patient while the other two go on to the staff camp. This group should take the following:

1. Map with location of patient marked and a compass.
2. Sun/insect protection
3. Water
4. Rain gear
5. First aid kit
6. Pocket knife
7. Lighter/matches
8. Food
9. Watch
10. Let the crew know where you are going.

Fire

Fire is a very real threat to Philmont; one spark could ignite an entire forest. Drought has existed for several years, leaving grasses and trees extremely dry. In 2002 the Ponil Complex fire began as three smaller fires triggered by lightening strikes and eventually burned over 90,000 acres of forest on Philmont, the Valle Vidal, and other private properties. Another large wildfire in 2006 burned just south of Philmont. In both cases, backcountry camps were closed and crew itineraries were rerouted.

Signs of fire can include flames, particles of ash in the air, and seeing or smelling smoke. If you see smoke, determine it's location by shooting a compass bearing. Identify your location on the map using grid coordinates and the probable location of the smoke. Make a note of what the smoke looks like, is it white or dark? Is there a specific point the smoke is coming from, or does it stretch over a wide area? Can you see flames, and are the flames on the ground or in the trees?

Report fires to the nearest staff camp. The staff will send out runners to confirm the location of the fire. Base Camp will coordinate with other backcountry camps to triangulate its position, and call out the Philmont Fire Department. When staying at a trail camp, a staff member may come by to warn you of imminent fire danger and evacuate your crew to the nearest staff camp or rendezvous point. Make sure to follow all staff directions, and to follow the prescribed fire plan, which is updated each year and issued with the crew paperwork in Base Camp.

If your crew is near a forest fire, do your best to avoid the flames and smoke. If possible, get behind the fire into the burn area, as all of the combustible material will be burnt. It may be necessary to abandon group and personal equipment in order to avoid fast-moving flames. Remember that the gear can always be replaced.

Suspicious Activity

If your crew encounters a person or you see activity that is suspicious, report it to the nearest staff camp. It is not unheard of for non-Philmont related people to trespass onto Philmont property. These include individuals who are by themselves, not wearing a Philmont staff uniform, or do not appear that they should be on Philmont property. Do not force a confrontation with these people.

Cell Phones

Cellular telephones have become an ever increasing sight in the backcountry since the technology has become cheaper, smaller, and with better coverage. Often crews may be tempted to call home from a mountaintop, or Advisors may try to check what is going on at work. Others bring cell phones as a means of contacting Base Camp in an emergency.

Aside from the aesthetics argument of technology in the backcountry, there are practical reasons why Philmont discourages taking cell phones on the trail. It is difficult to get a cell signal in many areas of the Ranch, especially in ravines or when surrounded by mountains. Batteries do not always hold a charge for ten days, and it is not possible to recharge electronic devices in the backcountry. The phone may cut off halfway through a call, so Base Camp may not get all of the information it needs, such as the exact location of the caller. Finally, users dial 911 instead of Philmont, which results in greater confusion. This is because a cell signal could be transmitted to a cell tower in Colorado, well outside of the Philmont area. Also, Philmont responds first to any emergencies on its property.

If you insist on carrying a cell phone, follow the guidelines that Philmont has spelled out regarding its use. When placing an emergency call, dial the main Philmont switchboard at (575) 376–2281. This number is monitored 24-hours a day during the summer. When you make the call, have all of the required emergency procedures information already written down. This will save time and the battery life of the cell phone. Give your expedition number, the name of the caller, the cell phone number, and state how much battery life you have left. Describe the situation clearly and quickly, and be prepared to give the camp name and site number or grid coordinates. Do not hang up until the staff member on the other end instructs you to do so.

There are some things you can do to protect your phone or to increase your chances of getting a signal. Keep your cell phone in a plastic bag to prevent moisture from damaging the electronics. You can even buy a small dry-box, which is used for rafting and sea kayaking, and is waterproof. Keep the battery close to you when its cold out, as cold temperatures drain the battery. When making a call, find the highest point that is safe to climb to get out a signal. Be aware that your battery may run down more quickly because of roaming.

Keep in mind that even if you are able to make a successful call to Base Camp, it can still take a long time for a response team to reach your location for evacuation. It can take up to two hours or more for staff from the nearest camp to get to a patient, and it can tack over two hours for a Search and Rescue (SAR) team to arrive from Base Camp. It can take many hours to evacuate a patient from the field and to transport to a hospital. You should be prepared to render First Aid until help arrives.

Training

Philmont requires that at least one person in the crew be certified in CPR and Wilderness First Aid. Proof of certification must be presented when checking in at Registration. There are also minimum participation standards that require that Scouts be either 14 years old or have completed the eighth grade. By this age everyone in the crew should have had some First Aid training by completing the First Aid merit badge or completing similar training in Venturing. Training provided by your Ranger builds on this general knowledge by reviewing the medical problems in the last chapter and teaching emergency procedures.

Because of the popularity of outdoor activities with the general public, there are now companies that specialize in outdoor emergency training. These programs offer courses for the layman outdoor enthusiast who wants to improve on his medical skills. Many of these programs offer a 2-day course in basic first aid that covers basic medical problems and how to report an emergency. The former is taught with an emphasis on how to utilize the equipment you have to treat patients, such as using foam pads as splinting material. The latter is important in that you learn the exact information a medical authority, such as a Search and Rescue team, would need to treat the patient. These training programs also focus on scenarios to practice these skills. Being able to treat and take care of a patient for an extended period of time is an essential component of these courses.

Philmont recommends that participants take the American Red Cross's 16-hour Wilderness First Aid Course to receive this more advanced training. The Philmont website provides more information on the Wilderness First Aid requirement and has a list of organizations that provide similar training.

Also, practice the skills you have learned before traveling to Philmont by staging a mock exercise with the crew. This exercise could be done as a troop activity, or during a crew shakedown hike. Remember, the more you put into your training at home, the more likely your will crew will have a successful trek.

Remember:

1. Copy the emergency procedures onto the crew map.
2. Send four calm people with their 10 essentials and patient information to the nearest staff camp when reporting an emergency.
3. Report forest fires or suspicious activity to the nearest staff camp.
4. Know Philmont's cell phone protocol and follow it when reporting an emergency.
5. Seek out training opportunities to improve your medical knowledge.

Soft Skills

"Soft skills" is the term referred to by Rangers that includes leadership development and group processing. These techniques are just as important to master as hard skills, and are a critical part of any successful trek. This section covers the different roles people perform in the crew, expeditionary behavior and group dynamics, the use of Thorns and Roses, and the crew duty roster.

Chapter 13: Crew Jobs

THERE ARE FOUR ROLES for participants in a Philmont crew. These are Advisor, Crew Leader, Chaplain's Aide, and Crew Member. Each role plays a vital function to the success of the crew and the trek.

Advisors

Philmont requires that each crew provide two adult leaders to accompany the crew on the trek. One advisor must be at least 18 years old, and the other must be at least 21 years old. If there are female participants, then there must be a female advisor who is at least 21 years old and a male advisor who is at least 21 years old.

The main responsibility of the advisors is to ensure the safety of the participants. Safety includes physical safety as well as emotional safety. Sometimes Scouts like to do things that may be too dangerous, such as crossing a stream when the water is too high and there is no bridge. Kids also may single out someone in the group to pick on, or make demeaning jokes. It is the Advisor's job to make sure that the Scouts stay on track and follow the Scout Oath and Scout Law.

Other than to maintain safety, all the Advisor has to do is to enjoy the trek, carry his/her share of group equipment, take lots of pictures, and provide words of wisdom and insight to the crew and crew leader. The crew and Crew Leader make most of the important decisions. It can be difficult for the Advisors to sit back and let things happen, but there are strategies that can be utilized to help them be effective but still keep the emphasis on the boys. More on this topic in the next chapter.

When recruiting group members for a Philmont crew, it is a good idea to have three Advisors. If one advisor must leave the crew during the trek for medical or other reasons, there will still be two Advisors left to continue the expedition.

Crew Leader

The Crew Leader is the Scout or Venturer that provides the day-to-day leadership for the crew, and helps to moderate Thorns and Roses in the evening. The Crew Leader may be either elected by the other crew members or is appointed to the position by an adult. It is preferable for the Crew Leader to be elected, as he/she will have greater legitimacy with the crew. There are not any prerequisites to being a Crew Leader, but some good benchmarks are a Scout that has attained at least Star rank and has been a Patrol Leader, Senior Patrol Leader, Venturing Vice President or President. Often the Crew Leader is someone who has been to Philmont before on a trek.

For the Crew leader, this may be the first time the participant has ever been in such a significant leadership position. Holding a troop/venturing crew position is helpful, but there are few experiences in Scouting where the youth is responsible for getting the group to camp, setting up camp, getting to program, making sure the meals are cooked, essentially all that is involved in an expedition. Back home in Boy Scout Troops or Venturing Crews, adults are often giving the orders, but at Philmont it is the Crew Leaders' responsibility.

Chaplain's Aide

The Chaplain's Aide is the Scout or Venturer in the crew designated to lead religious activities for the crew in the backcountry. These activities include daily readings from the Philmont devotional pamphlet *Eagles Soaring High*, leading the crew in the Philmont grace at mealtimes and the crew in prayer. The Chaplain's Aide also can help the Crew Leader with moderating Thorns and Roses in the evening, which will be discussed further in the next chapter. The crew member selected to be the Chaplain's Aide is also the moral officer of the crew, helping the Crew Leader and Advisors to keep spirits up when the days get tough. At the end of the trek the Chaplain's Aide certifies whether the crew has completed all the requirements for the Duty to God patch.

Crew Members

The Philmont trek can not happen without the crew. The crew members must do the camp chores, carry the food and gear, and cook the meals. It is important to learn how to be a leader, but it is more important to learn how to be part of a team that works well together and can accomplish the task at hand.

Duty Roster

The duty roster is a chart that divides up the typical camp chores, such as cooking, cleanup, water, and firewood. It is designed to divide up duties in a way that is equitable. This chart is filled out by the Crew Leader during Ranger Training.

All youth participants will be responsible for each job at least twice while on a trek. Sometimes this happens more often with smaller crews. Advisors are not typically on the crew duty roster. However, sometimes Advisors will volunteer to be on the roster when there are a small number of people in the crew. Some advisors volunteer to cook dinner and do cleanup for the last night on the trail, as a way of saying thanks to the crew participants for doing all the work for the last nine days.
Remember:

1. Advisors are adult leaders who ensure the safety of the crew. One must be at least 18 years old and the other 21

years old. If there are female participants, then one adult leader must also
be female and at least 21 years old,
and the other adult leader is a 21 year
old male.

2. The Crew Leader is the youth leader
   elected or appointed by the crew. They
   provide the day-to-day leadership for
   the crew to complete the trek.

3. The Chaplain's Aide provides spiritual
   guidance to the crew and leads Thorns
   and Roses.

4. Crew members work with the crew
   leadership to complete the trek.

5. The duty roster includes cooking,
   cleanup, water, and firewood.

Chapter 14: Group Dynamics

A LOT CAN HAPPEN in ten days. Crews that were dysfunctional before arriving to Philmont will learn how to work together as a team and achieve common goals. Sometimes crews that worked together at home, where everyone is best friends, become unglued in the backcountry. It is likely that there will be some kind of conflict within the crew, whether relatively minor or major, that will require processing.

Expeditionary Behavior

To better understand how a group behaves in a backcountry setting, we need to discuss expeditionary behavior. These are the behaviors exhibited by individuals and the group as a whole that affect the performance of the group throughout the trek. There are professionals that devote their lives to studying expeditionary behavior.

There are four stages of expeditionary behavior that a group can exhibit while on a trek. The first level is called the Honeymoon Stage. This is when group participants first meet each other and get to know each other. For most expeditions, this happens the first few days participants are on a course. Everyone is trying to get to know everyone else and understand the rules of their new environment. Group members generally are on their best behavior.

For Philmont participants, this stage begins at home at the troop or council contingent meetings, when everyone meets for the first time and starts building a relationship as a crew. For some crews that come from individual troops, the Scouts may have already known each other for years and have spent many nights out on troop campouts and summer camp.

The second level is the Building Block Stage. This is where participants begin learning how to work together as a team. For Philmont participants crews can reach this stage by the end of Ranger training. After the Ranger leaves, the crew no longer has someone to ask questions or to do things, the crew is on their own.

The Conflict Stage, is the next level. This is where the crew experiences conflict, for one reason or another. Perhaps Camper Jimmy isn't doing his assigned chores. Camper Timmy is being obnoxious by making jokes at the expense of others. Advisor Bob may insist the crew does things his way. We'll discuss more on conflict later in this chapter.

The Eureka Stage, is when the crew is functioning smoothly as a team. Everyone knows what his job is and gets it done. The crew is essentially firing on all pistons,

Keep in mind that some crews may be stuck on one stage, skip another, or never reach the Eureka Stage. They may be stuck in Conflict for the whole trek, arguing the entire time. Or maybe they skip Conflict and go straight to Eureka. Each crew is unique, with its own group culture, norms, and conflicts.

Crew Conflict

As mentioned above, there are numerous reasons conflict can occur in the crew. Here are some common reasons why crew members argue amongst themselves.

Not Making Program

Crews that are constantly late will feel discouraged, as they may miss out on an entire program slot. For instance, if you are twenty minutes late for horse rides at Beaubien, your crew may be out of luck, as another crew that was on standby may now have your slot. After a few days of missing program, tempers can boil.

Participants may blame others in the crew for lateness. Camper Johnny can't get his gear organized, leaving smellables down and keeping the crew behind to get stuff in order. Or the whole crew may be slow in getting their camp organized and the smellables secured.

Getting Lost

Sometimes crews take the wrong fork in the trail, or do not read the map correctly. In the Valle Vidal, crews can hike cross-country to get to their destination. If the crew Navigator does not shoot his bearings correctly, the crew could wind up way off course. This can be frustrating if the crew needs to be at a camp by a certain time. If it is late in the day, crew members will be cranky, hungry, and thirsty as well. Plus not everyone likes to hike extra miles, especially if it is in the wrong direction. Some Rangers joke that it does not matter to them where the crew hikes as they don't mind hiking all day!

Food

Food is a touchy subject in the backcountry, probably because it is one of the few creature comforts one has. Naturally, everyone wants a well cooked meal after a hard day of hiking. But at some point along the trek someone will accidentally knock the dinner pot over, causing that spaghetti dinner to spill all over the ground. Eating food with dirt particles in it is no fun, and the crews' anger will be directed at the hapless offender. Burning dinner is also a big no-no for the cooks.

In some cases, crews will be short meal bags. This is because nobody double-checked to make sure the crew had all of their meal bags issued from the commissary.

Before bagging up all that food, count it when it's still on the table.

Personal Habits

An individual's personal habits can get on other people's nerves. Someone's grooming habits, or lack thereof, is an example. A crew member may pass gas a lot. Or maybe Johnny's jokes are funny to Johnny, but are not that funny to the rest of the group.

Finding Smellables

It is not uncommon for crews to forget to hang up all of their smellables or to do an adequate campsite check before going to program or bedding down for the night. It is always aggravating for the crew to have a staff member inform them that they left smellables down from the bear bags. One time I walked past a site at Rich Cabins during the evening cow milking program. Half the crew had gone to milk the cow, while the other half had gone to hang smellables. Between the two groups, no one thought to take the big black bag of trash sitting right in the middle of camp! No one thought to ask who would take care of the garbage.

Crew Leader

The Crew Leader can be a major source of conflict for the group. Maybe the Crew

Leader who was the popular choice back home is turning out not to be the best organizer or leader in the backcountry. The Crew Leader could be too bossy, thinking that he/she can just order people around. Maybe the Crew Leader is forgetful. I have seen several Crew Leaders frantically search their packs for the Crew Leader's Copy which was left in the last staff camp. Remember, that piece of paper is your life! It is the record of travel for the crew throughout Philmont, and documents which staff camps are visited, completion of the conservation project, and whether the crew is signed up for burros/horses.

Sometimes, the Crew Leader was appointed by the head Advisor, who also happens to be the father of the Crew Leader. This can result in not only Advisor-Crew Leader conflict, but also Father-Son conflict.

Psychological Issues

Individuals in the crew often bring their own personal issues to Philmont, which can be accentuated while on the trail. Participants may have been diagnosed with psychological conditions such as ADHD, bipolar disorder, or others. Many of these conditions are treatable with medication. However, sometimes participants take a "medication holiday" during the summer months when not in school. This results in behavior that can seem erratic and unusual, and may cause a disruption in the crew.

Before you leave home for Philmont, check the medical forms for everyone in the crew for any conditions that may be a problem. Talk with the participant and his/her parents confidentially about the participants' treatment plan. They can talk to their physician about Philmont and how that may affect treatment.

During the trek the Scout may open up about a personal issue that he is experiencing, or certain behaviors may be observed by the crew during everyday interactions on the trail. If you have a concern, talk to the staff at the nearest staff camp to arrange a Chaplain visit. They are very helpful and are a great resource.

Advisors

The Advisors, or an individual Advisor, also can be a major source of conflict. The reasons vary, but here are a few key examples. One, Advisors can not let go. Many Advisors are adult leaders in the troop or council back home, and may hold jobs that require leadership and responsibility. They are used to giving orders and having control over the situation. On the trail, they fall into the same habits, telling the Scouts what to do. At Philmont, it is the Scouts who are making most of the decisions, and it is tough to control factors such as the weather, people's physical ability, etc. One of the strengths of Philmont is that the program is designed to promote leadership and teamwork amongst the Scouts and Venturers.

Second, Advisors are not physically fit enough to complete the trek. Even those Advisors that took the time to work out may find that after a few days of hiking they wished they had trained more. For those that are used to sedentary lifestyles, it can be a real struggle. There also are some Advisors who think they can handle a trek at 60 or 70 years old. Granted, there are those Advisors who are tough as nails at any age and can hike fifteen-year-olds into the ground, but others do not realize that their body isn't the same as it used to be. These factors result in very slow hiking speeds, which can be a source of conflict. I knew one crew that had an Advisor that hiked a mile an hour, which meant the whole crew hiked a mile an hour. On a 12-mile day, that's a lot of time on the trail.

Third, Advisors are not used to the hard living of backpacking for 10 days. They may be used to the creature comforts of home, eating solid food with a fork, and having access to electronic devices and flushing toilets. A Philmont expedition may be the first time they have ever camped without these luxuries.

Fourth, Advisors may have outdated concepts on Scouting. Philmont has had female staff almost since day one, and has had female field staff and managers for over forty years. Each summer their work is a vital contribution to the Philmont mission and the crews they lead. An Advisor who behaves in a disrespectful manner to any staffer or participant is not acting according to the Scout Oath or Law.

The fifth point is that Advisors do not know how to advise. I like to think that the Advisor is the wise sage of the group, the one who knows the questions but does not provide all the answers. In our modern society we seem to put more emphasis on technical knowledge versus wisdom. Thus, adults arriving at Philmont may not have the tools they need adequately guide the crew.

In case you haven't noticed, the lengthiest discussion of sources of conflict is Advisors. Every Philmont staffer has their share of horror stories of Advisors, but usually it is these stories that stand out the most. It's easy to forget that 99% of Advisors do an excellent job for their crews. Problems that arise on a trek are usually due to a lack of knowledge. Hence the purpose of this book, to help Philmont adult leaders to be better educated of these issues.

Resolving Conflict

There is no magic bullet for resolving conflict, but there are options available to the crew.

Thorns and Roses

Thorns and Roses is a Philmont tradition in its own right. Every night before bedtime the crew gathers around the fire ring in a circle. Each person in the crew talks about his Thorns, the things that he did not like that day, and Roses, the things he did like. There's also Buds, things that one is looking forward for tomorrow. There are a few rules to Thorns and Roses. Everyone has to be able to see each other, preferably sitting. Each person has an opportunity to speak honestly, and without interruption or criticism for other group members. When speaking of Thorns, do not single out an individual. For example, "I am frustrated that we take a long time hiking because Jimmy is too slow." A better way to express the emotion is, "I am frustrated that it takes us a long time to get to camp."

Once everyone has had a chance to speak his Thorns and Roses, the crew can continue discussion if there is a pressing topic critical to the group. For instance, if someone mentioned during Thorns and Roses about how the group gets out of camp late, the crew can brainstorm ideas on how to be more efficient. The idea is that there is an environment that is safe where everyone can express what they're feeling without being criticized or put-down. This also is an opportunity for the crew to plan out what time they want to wake up tomorrow, who is doing which chores, what time they need to get out of camp, and other matters.

Thorns and Roses is the best tool your crew can utilize to address conflict, and also prevent conflict from occurring. The Crew Leader has the responsibility for moderating the Thorns and Roses discussion, and the Chaplain's Aide can help with the discussion. During the Crew Leader and Chaplain's Aide meeting in Base Camp they will receive information from the Rangers and Chaplains on how to conduct the discussion.

Advisor/Crew Leader Meeting

After Thorns and Roses has concluded, I as the Ranger like to meet with the Crew Leader and all the Advisors for a few minutes to discuss the day and any leadership issues that need to be addressed. I find this a great opportunity for the Advisors to do their job, to advise the Crew Leader on their perspectives and observations on how the crew is functioning. This maintains an open door of communication between the Crew Leader and Advisors.

Additional Resources

If you feel that the crew just is not resolving its issues, no matter how hard you try, there are additional resources at your disposal. First is your Ranger, if he/she is still with the crew. The Rangers represents the one Philmont staff group that spends the most time with your crew on the trek, and will have a better idea as to how the group functions than someone stepping in from outside the group.

Next are the Backcountry staff. When staying at a staff camp, ask to speak with the Camp Director. These staff supervisors have worked at Philmont for several seasons, and have excellent experience and training working with crews. Both the Rangers and Camp Directors can provide a fresh perspective for your crew, which may not have been considered before.

Another resource is the Philmont Chaplains. These clergymen represent the four faith traditions, Catholic, Protestant, Jewish, and LDS, that maintain chapels and ministries at Philmont. There is always one Chaplain on call to respond to a crew in need of support, regardless of denomination or faith. Some are professional counselors with many years experience.

Conflict as a Good Thing

If your group is experiencing conflict, look on the bright side. Without conflict or struggle, we cannot grow as individuals, or work as teams. There always will be disagreements among people, but if we can put those differences aside and work together, amazing things can happen. That's one of the best things your crew can take away from the Philmont experience. Just know that the Philmont staff is there to support your crew on its journey.

Attitude is Everything

There is something to be said for having a positive attitude. A positive attitude is great when things are going well, and is even more important when it is cold and raining out. It can also be a great resource when convincing Scouts to attend program.

Sometimes crews skip program because they are tired, or they think the program will be boring. There are so many programs available, from climbing spar poles, to shooting black powder rifles, or mountain biking, available on your trek. Your group has come such a long way and hiked so far, it would be a shame to miss out on these opportunities.

The crew also has an opportunity to perform service work with the Conservation Department. Aside from doing the "Good Turn Daily," doing such a project is a requirement for attaining the Philmont Arrowhead. Here, again, is another chance to participate, so bring a positive attitude to the work. Many Scouts reflect on their Conservation projects as the highlight of their trek. Some return years later as older Scouts, Staff, or Advisors, and hike the stretch of trail that they worked on during their trek.

Remember:

1. Four Stages of expeditionary behavior: Honeymoon Stage, Building Block Stage, Conflict Stage, Eureka! Stage.
2. Know the potential sources of conflict that a crew could encounter on the trail.
3. Practice Thorns and Roses each night to prevent and resolve conflict.
4. Utilize Rangers, Backcountry Staff, and Chaplains as resources to resolve conflict.
5. Attitude is Everything.

Chapter 15: Backcountry Camps

IF YOU CONSIDER THE MOUNTAINS of Philmont to be the cake, then the programs are the icing. There are a number of programs that your crew can choose for their trek. These programs include historical interpretation, western lore, shooting sports, and high adventure, which are delivered by the backcountry staff at various camps. There also are conservation programs available which allow crews to complete the necessary service hours to earn the Philmont Arrowhead. All of these programs contribute to making Philmont a unique outdoor experience.

The sun rises over the Tooth of Time.

This chapter reviews the different programs available and their requirements. We will also discuss the protocols when arriving in a staff camp and staying overnight.

Historical Interpretation

"Interp" programs recreate a certain period of time for crews to experience. The staff dress in period costumes, and adopt a character from that time period. Interp programs include homesteading, mountain-main living, mining, logging, and Mexican homesteading. What's exciting about these programs is that crews get to be a part of the everyday life of the camp. For instance, you can help milk the cow at Rich Cabins, or cut railroad ties at Crater Lake. There are also historical programs that tell the story of Waite Phillips. These include Fish Camp and the Hunting Lodge.

Western Lore

Although the staff at western lore camps dress as cowboys, they do not deliver a historical program. Instead, the staff at Ponil, Clarks Fork, and Beaubien interpret how a modern-day cowboy camp operates. Program includes horseback riding, branding, lassoing and horseshoe toss games, and a chuckwagon dinner and evening campfire program.

Shooting Sports

Shooting Sports camps include Harlan, which does shotgun shooting, and Sawmill, which specializes in 30.06 rifle shooting. Both programs allow crews to load ammunition. Black Mountain, Clear Creek, and Miranda shoot black powder muzzeloading rifles.

High Adventure

This covers a variety of programs, including rock climbing and rappelling, mountain biking, search-and-rescue, challenge course, GPS navigation, astronomy, environmental awareness, and more.

Conservation

Conservation programs are available at certain staff camps during the summer, and there usually are at least two conservation sites for crews to choose from on any given trek. Usually the Conservation staff are based at the staff camp, and the actual worksite is some distance out of camp, sometimes several miles. Projects include building trail, preventing erosion, and wildfire restoration.

Advisors Coffee

Each evening, staff camps hold an Advisors Coffee hour. It is meant to be an opportunity for the Advisors to have some time away from the crew to enjoy fellowship with other Advisors, learn about the next days

hike, or receive important announcements from Philmont, such as regarding fire dangers. Coffee and hot water are served, as well as cookies or some other snack.
Arriving in Camp

When arriving in a staff camp, the crew must check-in at the staff cabin. To do this, the whole crew should make their way to the cabin. Once at the cabin, the crew leader should step up to the porch to notify the staff that the crew has arrived. The staff will invite the crew up to the porch for the "Porch Talk." This talk, oftentimes performed in a humorous manner, introduces the crew to the camp and informs them of what is available.

The crew leader must have the Crew Leader's Copy in hand for the porch talk. The staff member will enter the crew number, itinerary, and where the crew is from into the camp logbook. Next, the staffer will begin the porch talk. He/she will tell the crew the following information:

- Programs available and program times. Includes
  - Day programs
  - Evening programs
  - Advisor's Coffee.
- Conservation projects available.
- What to bring to program.
- Location of water sources.
- Swap Box availability.
- Location of trash can.
- Mail

- Bear safety in camp.
- Other safety concerns in camp.

Once the porch talk is completed, the crew is shown to their campsite by the staffer. He/she will point out the location of the fire ring, sump, and bear cable. If in the Valle Vidal, the staffer may walk the crew to the designated area and may suggest where to place the camp.

What to Bring to Program

When attending program, it is recommended that each participant bring a quart of water, raingear, and closed-toe shoes. Some programs require specific equipment. For instance, long pants are needed for horseback rides and spar pole climbing. Conservation work requires long pants, raingear, two quarts of water, food for snacking, the crew leader's copy, and all participants and Advisors.

Crew Behavior In Camp

When in camp it is important that the crew members are on their best behavior. There are a few simple things that the crew can do to promote positive relations with the backcountry staff while in camp.

It's Their Home

The staff who work in the backcountry live at these camps for the whole summer. Visiting the camp is like staying at someone's house. Respect designated staff areas, such as sleeping quarters. During mealtime, stay off the cabin porch. Do not deface camp facilities, such as latrine walls.

Show Up on Time

Do your best to get to program on time. Some camps have designated program times, such as rock climbing camps, while others have open program times, which means that the crew can come to do program whenever it is available. Missing even the first ten minutes of program means the crew misses important safety information, and in some cases, miss program altogether. Note that program times for horseback rides are made in Base Camp. The western lore camps will be expecting your crew at the designated time.

Do Expect High Standards

Philmont invests a lot of time and energy to train its staff to deliver a high-quality program to participants, and to provide excellent customer service. You, as the customer, should expect the highest standards in service from the staff. You should not tolerate rude or inappropriate behavior. At the end of the trek, crews will complete evaluations of Philmont, including Backcountry camps. These evaluations are read by the Director of Program for Philmont, as well as senior seasonal staff supervisors. Philmont takes this documentation seriously as a means to improve its performance.

Don't Expect Everything

Although trained to provide cheerful, friendly customer service, the staff can not do everything. Some requests can and will be fulfilled, especially medical treatment. But there are some things that the staff can not do. One is to allow an itinerary change based on the desire to stay at a different camp for convenience. An example is changing the itinerary from Clarks Fork to Tooth Ridge Camp. Everyone wants to have the experience of being on the Tooth of Time for sunrise, but the sites at Tooth Ridge Camp are filled every night due to the demand. Consequently, staying at a different staff camp or trail camp that is off of the itinerary is also unacceptable, and could result in serious consequences for the crew.

Another common request is early program. Some camps may accommodate early programs for crews that were rained out the previous day. However, there is no guarantee. Check with the staff camp for what is available. Nor is there a guarantee that a crew passing through camp can participate in program, as crews that are staying at that camp often have first priority. Again, check with the staff.

Sometimes crews pack too much stuff with them into the backcountry. Oftentimes they try to mail back extra food and equipment. These kinds of requests cannot be accommodated by Philmont, as space is limited on vehicles. Also, Philmont does not want to

The Tooth of Time, one of Philmont's most recognizable features.

be responsible for these items. The philosophy is, "if you hiked out with it, you hike back with it."

There are only two camps on all of Philmont where crews cannot deposit garbage or drop mail. These camps are Crooked Creek and Black Mountain, which are primitive living camps. There are no roads leading to these camps, and no purified running water. French Henry also lacks purified water.

Other Crews

Most camps have several crews, sometimes a dozen or more, staying the night. They expect that other crews behave within the standards of the BSA. Being loud, rude, or other unacceptable behavior leaves others with a poor impression of your crew.

Backcountry programs can be the highlight of a crew's experience at Philmont. Whichever camp you stay at, remember to take advantage of all the opportunities to do program. It's all part of the Philmont experience!

Remember

1. Historical interpretation, high adventure, shooting sports, western lore, and conservation programs are available at backcountry camps.
2. When arriving in a staff camp check-in at the cabin for the porch talk.
3. Bring a quart of water, closed-toe shoes and raingear to program. Some programs require additional equipment.
4. Be respectful of the staff while in camp, it is their home for the summer.
5. Show up to program on time or early.
6. Expect high standards of the backcountry staff. They are there for you.
7. Don't expect everything.
8. Take advantage of all the programming available.

Chapter 16: Other Philmont Opportunities

PHILMONT OFFERS MANY other treks and programs for those interested in a Philmont experience. Some are available to individuals, others are programs designed for crews, and there are positions for those interested in being Philmont staff. Check with Philmont for the most current program dates and prices.

Special Trek Programs

Rayado Trek

This is a 21-day program that emphasizes teamwork and leadership. Participants arrive as individuals to Philmont and are placed into provisional crews. Each crew has two Rangers that works with the crew throughout the trek. Participants must be between 15–20 years old and in good physical condition. Prior Philmont experience on a trek is helpful, but not required. There are two sessions each summer, one that begins in June, the second in July.

The Next Summit

The adventure doesn't have to end with the close of your trek. There are plenty of other opportunities available for those looking for challenge and opportunity.

Mountain Trek

This program is a 6-day trek for 14–20 year olds whose parents are participants at the Philmont Training Center. Each crew is assigned two Rangers for the week. Crews hike on a pre-determined itinerary that takes advantage of Backcountry programs. These treks leave weekly from the Philmont Training Center.

Trail Crew Trek

Trail Crew Trek is a new program that is 14-days long, and teaches participants trail construction techniques and familiarizes them with the William T. Hornaday Conserveration Award. Participants must be at least 16 years old.

Roving Outdoor Conservation School (ROCS)

ROCS is a 21-day program that emphasizes conservation work, wildfire ecology, bear ecology, and backpacking. Participants arrive as individuals and are placed into provisional crews under the leadership of two ROCS Instructors from the Philmont Conservation Department. Participants must be between 16–20 years old and in good physical condition. Prior Philmont experience is recommended but not required.

Order of the Arrow Trail Crew (OATC)

OATC is designed for members of the Order of the Arrow. Participants perform seven days of conservation work, then get a seven day trek. They are led by two foremen from the Conservation Department. Scouts must be at least 16 years old, in good physical condition, and be recommended from their Order of the Arrow lodges.

Cavalcade Treks

Cavalcades are 8-day horse packing trips organized through the Philmont Ranch Department. Crews from troops or crews are selected through a lottery drawing on January 18th. Scouts/Venturers and their Advisors learn how to saddle, ride, and take care of horses. They also get to play the role of the Western cowboy during their trek. Cavalcades hit the trail several times a year under the direction of two Philmont Horsemen/Wranglers. Programs start throughout the summer.

Ranch Hands

Participants in this program work as cattle ranch hands for eight days, then get an eight day Cavalcade trek. Operated by the Philmont Ranch Department, participants must be at least 16 years old and have some experience working with horses.

National Advanced Youth Leadership Experience (NAYLE)

NAYLE is a leadership training program designed for youth leaders responsible for conducting leadership training in their home councils. Potential participants must be at least 14 years old and have completed a similar program at the council level. There are six, 1-week sessions held each summer at Rocky Mountain Scout Camp.

Philmont Training Center

As part of his gift to Philmont, Waite Phillips included his summer home and grounds, the Villa Philmonte. The Boy Scouts converted this building into the Philmont Training Center. Each summer, the PTC welcomes adult leaders for a week of training and Scouting fellowship. Courses include BSA high adventure, district leadership, and Scouting in the LDS Church. Attendees may bring their spouse, children, or a friend of the child, who can participate in a variety of group programs that are age appropriate and the Mountain Trek program.

Off-Season Programs

Just because it isn't summer doesn't mean you can't go to Philmont! Philmont operates several off season programs for people to participate in.

Autumn Adventure

This program occurs in the Fall from September to the end of October. Crews organize themselves at home and reserve a slot. When they arrive at the Ranch they are assigned a Guide for the duration of the trip. Crews get to select their own itineraries and can spend as little as a weekend on the trail or much longer. There are no Backcountry programs available. Participants must be at least 14 to participate. This is the only time an entire crew of adults can hike at Philmont.

Kanik

This is Philmont's winter program. Crews assembled at home get to learn how to camp and survive in the winter. Activities include cross-country skiing, building quinzees, snowshoeing, and sledding. Campers must be at least 14 years old to participate. Crews pay by the day, with many staying for an extended weekend, or longer during spring break.

Philbreak

An alternative spring break program, Philbreak is meant for potential Philmont staff between 18 and 25. Participants spend a week performing service projects on the Ranch, staying in Base Camp and driven to the worksite each day. They also get to spend two days camping with the Kanik program.

Double H High Adventure Base

Philmont began operation of the Double H in 2004 as part of an agreement with the Rocky Mountain Elk Foundation. Crews hike with a guide on a 100,000 acre ranch near Datalis, New Mexico. Programs include cross country desert backpacking, astronomy, flora/fauna, and black powder rifle shooting. The Double H is an exciting program for those who want a New Mexico backpacking experience but find it difficult to reserve a spot at Philmont. The season runs from mid-June to early August.

Staff Opportunities

Each year Philmont must recruit, hire, and train over 1,000 people to work at the Ranch. Jobs are available in Base Camp, Rangers, Conservation, Backcountry, the Philmont Training Center, museums, and

Double H staff. Staff must be at least 18 years old and be able to provide a completed medical form and paperwork. Some positions require the applicant to be 21 and the ability to drive a vehicle. Although most staff are college students on summer break, there are many staff who are "older and bolder," such as teachers, professors, business owners, and retirees.

Working at Philmont is a rewarding experience that allows you to be a part of the flagship camp for the Boy Scouts of America and the largest youth camp in the world. Staff have the opportunity to join the Philmont Staff Association, as well as return to the Ranch in the off season for the annual New Year's celebration as well as Philbreak, Philmont's version of alternative spring break.

Remember

1. Special summer treks and programs include: Rayado, Mountain Trek, ROCS, OATC, Cavalcades, and the Philmont Training Center.
2. Off-season programs include Autumn Adventure, Kanik, Philbreak and the Philmont Training Center.
3. The Double H is an exciting alternative to hiking at Philmont.
4. Over 1, 000 staff are hired each summer to work Philmont programs.

Conclusion

PHILMONT IS A ONCE-IN-A-LIFETIME adventure for many Scouts and Scouters. On the trail, crew members have the opportunity to put into practice the skills that they have learned as Scouts, and to put into practice new skills learned from their Ranger. For the leaders, both young and adult, Philmont is the ultimate test of Scouting leadership developed over many years in the troop or venture crew. In addition, the physical challenges of hiking long distances, climbing mountains, and carrying heavy loads can test the strength of each crew member. It is no wonder then, that Philmont is called the summit of Scouting.

A Philmont expedition can seem like a daunting task for anyone, especially for one who has never been there before. In this book I have tried to provide a clearer picture as to what the experience is like and the preparations necessary to have a positive Philmont experience.

This book is but one of many resources available to you, such as visiting Philmont-related websites, of which a list appears in the Appendices. Also, talk to others who have been to Philmont, and who can provide helpful tips from their experiences. Finally, when you get to Philmont, ask your Ranger.

He/she will have the most up-to-date information available.

Philmont has been a very important part of who I am. On its trails I have learned new things about myself, and have made many friends. It is one of the defining experiences of my life which I shall always treasure for as long as I live. I hope that you will find in its mountains some of the same meaning that I have. For me, Philmont will always be, "Heaven on Earth."

Bibliography

Herrero, Stephen. Bear Attacks: Their Causes and Avoidance. Globe Pequot Press, 1985.

Schimelpfenig, Tod. *Wilderness Medicine.* National Outdoor Leadership School. Stackpole Books, 2000.

Stuever, Mary and Daniel Shaw. *Philmont Field Guide.* Philmont Scout Ranch. Cimarron, NM, 1985.

Guidebook to Adventure. Philmont Scout Ranch. Cimarron, NM.

Philmont Ranger Field Book. Philmont Scout Ranch. Cimarron, NM.

Appendices

Appendix A
Equipment Lists

These lists have been adapted from the *Philmont Guidebook to Adventure*. If necessary, many of the items listed below can be purchased or rented at Philmont.

Personal

Pack

- Backpack
- Pack cover

Sleep

- Sleeping bag with stuff sack
- Straps for sleeping bag
- Sleeping pad
- Ground cloth/tarp
- Sleep clothes

Clothing

- Well broken-in hiking boots
- Wool socks (2–3 pairs)
- Liner socks (3 pair)
- Underwear (2–3 changes)
- Hiking shorts (2 pair)
- t-shirts (2 pair)

- Long sleeve shirt
- Warm sweater or sweatshirt made of wool/synthetic
- Lightweight jacket/windbreaker
- Rain jacket and pants
- Sun hat

Eating

- Deep bowl
- Cup
- Spoon
- Water bottles (at least 2 quarts)

Personal

- Small pocketknife
- Matches or lighter
- 50' 1/8-inch nylon cord
- Flashlight/headlamp
- Compass
- Bandannas/handkerchiefs (2)
- Whistle
- Money ($10-$20 in small bills)
- Small towel
- Note pad and pen
- Sunglasses

Personal Smellables

- Smellables bag

- Toothpaste
- Toothbrush
- Personal medications
- Lip Balm
- Band-aids
- Moleskin/Molefoam
- 1" adhesive tape
- Biodegradable camp soap
- Tampons/sanitary napkins
- Sunscreen at least SPF 15
- Extra film
- Batteries
- Disposable cameras
- Foot powder
- Insect repellent
- Wet wipes

Optional

- Camera-non disposable
- Watch
- Fishing equipment/license
- Pre-stamped postcards
- Rubber bands
- Long underwear
- Shaving equipment
- *Philmont Fieldguide*

Group Gear

Provided by Philmont

- Nylon dining fly 12x12'

- Collapsible poles for fly
- Philmont backpacker nylon tent
- Trail chef kits
- 8-quart pot6-quart pot with lid
- 4-quart pot with lid4-quart pot with lid
- 1 fry pan with handle1 fry pan with handle
- Large aluminum spoon
- Spatula
- Sump Frisbee
- Hot pot tongs
- Extra 8-quart or 6-quart pot for washing dishes
- Plastic trash bags
- Biodegradable soap
- Scrub pads
- Zip-lock bags
- Water purification
- 2 150' bear bag ropes
- Bear bags

Provided by the Crew

- Philmont overall map and sectionals
- 8 tent stakes per person: 12–14 per tent, 10 for dining fly.
- Water containers suitable for backpacking
- Lightweight stoves
- Fuel bottles and funnel
- First Aid Kit
- Spices
- Padlock for crew lockers

- Measuring cup (can use a personal cup)

Appendix B
Leave No Trace

Seven Principles

1) Plan ahead and prepare.
2) Travel and camp on durable surfaces.
3) Dispose of waste properly.
4) Leave what you find.
5) Minimize campfire impact.
6) Respect wildlife.
7) Be considerate of other visitors.

For more information, visit Leave No Trace at www.lnt.org.

Philmont Wilderness Pledge

Through good Scout camping, I pledge to preserve the beauty and splendor of the Philmont Wilderness.

I commit myself to:

1. An absence of litter and graffiti.
2. Respect for Philmont's wildlife.
3. Conservation and proper use of water.
4. Respect for trails and trail signs.
5. Proper use of campsites.

Appendix C
Philmont Resources on the Internet

Philmont Official Website:
www.scouting.org/philmont

Official website maintained by the Boy Scouts of America. Contains descriptions of all Philmont programs, links to download application forms, and tips for participants.

Philmont Unofficial Website:
www.philmont.com

Maintained by former Philmont staffer Jay Jolicoeur, contains a message board for Philmont participants to post questions.

Selden's List of Philmont Webpages:
www.lns.cornell.edu/~seb/philmont.html

Maintained by Selden Ball, this site contains links to many Philmont-related webpages, trail journals, and photo albums. Not all links are active.

Tooth of Time Traders:
www.toothoftimetraders.com

Philmont's trading post website. Contains a wide selection of equipment, clothing, Philmont novelites, and Boy Scout/Venturing items.

Philmont Staff Association:
www.philstaff.com

Official website for the PSA, with information on how to become a member, reunions, photos, and special projects.

Philring:
philring.anvilheadproductions.com

An association of Philmont-related websites maintained by former Philmont Ranger Jason Cotting.

Appendix D
Contact Information

Philmont Contact

Philmont Scout Ranch
17 Deer Run Road
Cimarron, NM 87714
(575) 376–2281

Website:
www.philmont.com

Appendix E
Common Philmont Terms

Admin: Short for Administration, this area houses offices for upper Philmont management. Nearby are the Philmont commissary and motor pool.

Advisor: Adult leader for the crew. There must be one Advisor who is at least 18 years old, and another at least 21 years old. If there are female participants, then there must be one female Advisor who is at least 21 years old and one male Advisor who is at least 21 years old.

Air-Traffic Controller: Also known as the "Tinker Toy." This is the small plastic piece that connects the two front poles in a Philmont tent.

Backcountry Staff: The Philmont staff who works at a backcountry camp and facilitate programming for the crew.

Bear Bags: Plastic feed bags used by crews to hang food and smellables.

Bear Cables: Steel cables bolted to trees and high enough off the ground to allow crews to hang their smellables.

Bearmuda Triangle: The fire ring, sump, and bear cable. These are the most likely places a bear will detect smellables.

Chaplain's Aide: A youth participant designated by the crew to provide spiritual inspiration throughout the trek. Keeps track of the crews' progress towards obtaining the Duty to God award.

CHQ: Short for Camping Headquarters, this is where Philmont's base facilities are located, including the Welcome Center, Registration, Logistics, Services, Security, News and Photo, the chapels, and the tent cities. Also known as "Base."

Crew Leader: The youth leader designated by the crew to lead them throughout the trek. Runs Thorns and Roses.

Crew Leader's Copy: The piece of paper that lists the itinerary for the crew. Is presented to backcountry camps for check-in, and is needed for signing off on the crews' conservation project. Do not lose it, it's your life

Conservationist: The Philmont staffer who oversees a backcountry conservation site and signs off on the crews' conservation project.

Duty to God Award: A religious award that Philmont participants can earn while on the trail.

Expedition Number: The number that identifies the crew. For instance, a contingent might be identified as 620F. If that contingent has four crews, then they will be identified as 620F1–4.

Fire Ring: The cooking area in a campsite, marked by a metal ring.

Five W's: Wind, Water, Wildlife, Widowmakers, and Weather. Used as a guideline for setting up tents.

Four T's: Touch, Turn, Trust, Tinkle. The four things you shouldn't do to a trail sign.

Itinerary Number: The number that identifies the trek the crew is completing. Usually there are two crews at the most per trek per day. So two crews that are on itinerary 5 will be identified as 5 A/B.

Meal Bags: The plastic bags that contain the Philmont trail meals.

Mini-Bears: Refers to squirrels and chipmunks. They can get a hold of food just as easily as a big-bear.

Navigator: The crew member responsible for the map and compass. This job is rotated among each person in the crew over the course of the trek.

Number Block: Identifies the site number for a particular campsite, usually nailed to a tree.

Pacesetter: The crew member responsible for setting a comfortable hiking pace for the rest of the crew. One person can have this job, or it can be rotated among the rest of the crew.

Philmont Arrowhead Award: The award earned by participants that complete a Philmont

Trek: Designed after the Arrowhead rock formation on the North Slope of Tooth of Time Ridge.

Pilot-to-Bombardier: Backcountry latrines with two seats placed opposing each other, so that two users sit back-to-back. Do not have walls.

Pilot-to-Copilot: Backcountry latrines with two seats placed side-by-side and do not have walls.

Porch Talk: The check-in process for a crew when it arrives in a backcountry staff camp.

Ranger: The Philmont staffer who is with the crew for its first four days at Philmont and teaches the crew all the necessary skills to have a successful trek.

Red Roof Inn: Backcountry latrines that have a roof and are surrounded by a wall.

RO: Short for the Ranger Office.

Smellables: Denotes anything that is made by man and has a smell. Includes food, trash, toiletry items, sump strainer and spatula, empty bear bags, clothes with food stains or odors, and blood.

Sump: Used to drain dishwater, is made of PVC plastic with a metal screen. Most sumps have a rubber neck which allow the top part it to pop off the sump if knocked over by a bear.

Sump strainer: A piece of plastic issued by Philmont to strain large food particles from dishwater over the sump. It and the rubber scraper are considered smellables and must be hung in the bear bags at night.

Swap Box: Boxes at backcountry camps where crews can either deposit unopened food packages or pick up some extra food.

Thorns and Roses: The daily debriefing session held by the crew each night on the trail. The thorns are the things that went well, and roses the things that could have been better. Also included are buds, what you are looking forward for tomorrow.

Yum-Yums: Food particles leftover from the dishwashing and straining process.

Yum-Yum Bag: A resealable plastic bag used to scrap Yum-Yums into and stored in the bear bags at night. Can be disposed of at staff camps that accept trash.

About the Author

Bill Sassani has served on the Philmont staff for ten summers as a Ranger, Mountain Trek Ranger, Rayado Ranger, Ranger Trainer, Service Academy Coordinator, and backcountry Camp Director at Urraca, Miner's Park, and Whiteman Vega. He has extensive experience training crews for their Philmont adventure, as well as supervising other Philmont staff. Outside of Philmont Bill has worked for several outdoor education organizations. He is an Eagle Scout who holds a master's degree in outdoor education. This is his first book.

CPSIA information can be obtained
at www.ICGtesting.com
Printed in the USA
BVHW02s2237101217
502437BV00001B/5/P